I0418689

No Sabo
Spanish Phrasebook

800 Spanglish Phrases to Keep You From Just Smiling and Nodding

Includes essential vocabulary, phrases and real-life examples for Latinos

Explore to Win

© 2026 Explore To Win LLC

All rights reserved

© 2026 Explore To Win LLC. All rights reserved.

No part of this publication may be reproduced, distributed, or transmitted in any form or by any means, including photocopying, recording, or other electronic or mechanical methods, without the prior written permission of the copyright owner, except in the case of brief quotations used in reviews or noncommercial uses permitted by copyright law.

Unauthorized use may constitute copyright infringement and intellectual property violations. Such actions may result in civil and criminal liability, including but not limited to statutory damages, attorney's fees, and legal costs, as permitted under applicable law.

This book is intended solely for personal, non-commercial use. You may not modify, sell, or publicly share any content from this publication without written consent.

Disclaimer:
The content in this book is for educational purposes only and does not constitute legal, financial, or medical advice. Readers should consult qualified professionals before acting on any information contained herein. The publisher disclaims liability for any loss incurred as a result of the use of this material.

Explore To Win LLC reserves the right to enforce its intellectual property rights to the fullest extent of the law.

Table of Contents

JOIN OUR FREE SPANISH COMMUNITY

TO SOUND MORE NATURAL, LEARN FROM EXPERTS, AND LISTEN TO ALL THE PHRASES NARRATED VIA AN AUDIBLE FREE TRIAL!

SCAN THE QR CODE

— OR —

visit **bit.ly/4sUdr6f**

Introduction:

Welcome to the *No Sabo* Club

We know that being Latino in an English-speaking country can be hard. Whether we're being too Latino or not Latino enough, we face constant scrutiny by others and ourselves. We feel you and know exactly what it's like!

Being a *no sabo* kid used to be something to be ashamed of, but today's generations are reclaiming the term and wear it as a badge of pride and relatable cultural marker of our Latino heritage. We know that you've probably been exposed to Spanish your entire life—whether it was your mom calling you *"mi amor"*, one of your *tías* asking about how you did *en la escuela,* or hearing *"ay, Dios mío"* while watching a *telenovela*—but you're here because you have a desire to communicate effortlessly with your Spanish-speaking family and friends, and that's exactly what this book is here to teach you!

Unlike other Spanish-teaching books, this one was made from scratch with you in mind! It was designed to give **you**—a Latino who has listened to Spanish their entire life—the confidence to speak Spanish fluently and feel included whenever it is spoken in your daily life.

And though your aim may be to surprise your *abuela* with your newly acquired Spanish-speaking skills, you should also know that learning Spanish is a great plus for other aspects of life, like work! After all, Spanish is the official language in 21 countries and has over 600 million speakers worldwide! So we strongly encourage you to embrace your roots and make the most of your Latino background by using Spanish to boost your life and work!

This book offers:

- **Phrases** for you to use in different Spanish-speaking contexts

- **Pronunciation guides** to gain the confidence to speak with anyone!

- **Cultural notes** on how or when to use certain phrases— and when not to!

- **Regional swaps** to tend to the Spanish variant you are trying to speak in!

- **Exercises** to practice what you've learned and fix the knowledge!

- **Challenges** for you to take your newly acquired language skills for a spin in real-life scenarios!

...and so much more!

Are you ready to join the *No sabo* club and embark on this Spanish-speaking journey?

Chapter 1:
Family Party Survival Kit

Greetings & Small Talk

Hola, ¿cómo estás? - Hi, how are you?
(OH-lah, KOH-moh es-TAHS)
😄 Smile — it buys you 3 extra seconds to think.

¡Qué gusto verte! - So nice to see you!
(KEH GOOS-toh BER-teh)
😄 Works for family or friends — instant warmth points.

¿Cómo está la familia? - How's the family?
(KOH-moh es-TAH lah fah-MEE-lee-ah)
😄 They'll think you're a pro conversationalist.

¡Tanto tiempo! - ¡It's been too long!
(TAHN-toh tee-EHM-poh)
😄 You can also add *sin verte* if you'd like:
¡Tanto tiempo sin verte! to say "Long time no see".

¡Cuánto has crecido! - How you've grown!
(koo-AHN-toh ahs kre-SEE-doh)
😄 Especially to tell little kids or something
your *tías* might say to you.

Te extrañé. - I've missed you.
(teh eks-trah-NYEH)

😄 You can add *tanto* to really win your *tía* over.

Ven a saludar a la abuela. - Come say hi to your grandma.
(behn ah sah-LOO-dahr ah lah ah-boo-EH-lah)
😄 This is something you might even hear from your *abuela*, talking about herself in the third person.

¡Dame un abrazo! - Give me a hug!
(DAH-me oon ah-BRAH-soh)
😄 If you're feeling a bit sassy, you could say ¿Dónde está mi abrazo? ("Where's my hug?")

¿Dónde está mi tía preferida? - Where's my favorite aunt?
(DOHN-deh ehs-TAH mee TEE-ah preh-feh-REE-dah)
😄 Especially if you have only one aunt, you'll make her smile for sure!

Tía's Questions and How to Answer Them

Estás muy flaco/flaca. ¿Estás comiendo bien? - You're so thin, are you eating well?
(ehs-TAHS mooy FLAH-koh/FLAH-kah. ehs-TAHS koh-mee-EHN-doh bee-ehn)
😄 Classic *tía*, worrying more than necessary!

Sí, estoy comiendo muy bien. - Yes, I'm eating very well.
(SEE es-TOH-ee koh-MYEHN-doh mooy bee-EN)
😄 Pat your stomach for drama.

Estás más gordo/gorda. - You look fatter.
(ehs-TAHS mahs GOHR-doh/GOHR-dah)
😄 It does sound harsh, but it is usually said out of love. They may also change *gordo* for **rellenito** which means "plumper".

¿No sabes que ya no se habla de los cuerpos ajenos, tía? - Don't you know we don't comment on other people's bodies anymore, aunt?

(noh SAH-behs keh ja noh seh AH-blah deh lohs KWEHR-po-
hs ah-heh-nohs, TEE-ah)
😄Add a smart smile so that you're aunt understands you
mean it as a joke (at least partially!)

¿Ya tienes novio/novia? - Do you already have a boyfriend/
girlfriend?
(jah tee-EH-nehs NOH-byoh/NOH-byah)
😄 With **ya**, your *tía* is implying that you should be getting one
soon!

¿Qué estás esperando para tener novio/novia? - What are
you waiting for to get a boyfriend/girlfriend?
(keh ehs-TAHS ehs-peh-RAHN-doh PAH-rah teh-NEHR NOH-
byoh/NOH-byah)
😄 Your aunt may be pushy on this one, but smile to diffuse
the tension and laugh it off!

¿Y el novio/la novia, para cuándo? - When will you have a
boyfriend/girlfriend?
(ee ehl NOH-byoh/lah NOH-bya PAH-rah KWAHN-doh)
😄 Yes, there are many ways in which she can ask the same
question, sometimes they use them all!

No tengo novio/novia todavía. - I don't have a boyfriend/
girlfriend yet.
(noh TEHN-goh NOH-byoh/NOH-byah toh-dah-BEE-ah)
😄 An awkward laugh may be the only way out of any
further variations of this question..

¿Para cuándo el casamiento? - When's the wedding?
(PAH-rah KWAHN-doh ehl kah-sah-MYEHN-toh)
😄 This doesn't necessarily imply you already have a
girlfriend or boyfriend, she just want you to get married!

Primero déjame conseguir novio/novia. - First let me get a
boyfriend/girlfriend.
(pree-MEH-roh DEH-hah-meh kohn-seh-GEER NOH-byoh/
NOH-byah)

13

😁 A risky answer. You might enter the "When will that be?" loop.

¿Tan linda y sin anillo? - So beautiful and no ring?
(tahn LEEN-dah ee seen ah-NEE-joh)
😁 Once you get a girlfriend, she may say this to her or, if you bring your boyfriend, she may say this to you in front of him!

¿Cuándo piensas formalizar las cosas? - When are you planning to make things official?
(KWAHN-doh pee-EHN-sahs fohr-mah-lee-SAHR lahs KOH-sas)
😁 "Making it official" would be to "put a ring on it" in this case—again with the marriage thing!

¿Cuándo nos vas a dar la sorpresa? - When are you going to surprise us?
(KWAHN-doh nohs bahs ah dahr lah sohr-PREH-sah)
😁 The "surprise" in question may be to get married or have a baby, you choose which one she's nodding at.

Mira que se te va a ir el tren... - You're gonna miss the train...
(MEE-rah keh seh teh bah ah eer ehl trehn)
😁 Yes, of course she's hinting at you missing the opportunity to have a baby or getting married!

Ya estás en edad, m'ijo/m'ija. - You're old enough, child.
(jah ehs-TAHS ehn eh-DAHD MEE-hoh/MEE-hah)
😁 Again with the getting married and having kids, by now you don't need to reply.

Tranquila, que no me voy a quedar para vestir santos. - I won't stay single forever.
(trahn-KEE-lah keh noh meh boy ah keh-DAHR PAH-rah be-hs-TEER SAHN-tohs)
😁 If a woman *se quedó para vestir santos*, it basically means that she's a spinster. Using this phrase will not only answer your *tía*'s questions, but also leave her in awe that you know it!

14

Si me sigues preguntando, nunca. - If you keep asking, never.

(see meh SEE-gehs preh-goon-TAHN-doh NOON-ka)

😄 Of course, it's meant as a joke! Add a pause between *preguntando* and *nunca* for a bit of suspense and drama!

¿Y los niños, para cuándo? - When will you have kids?

(ee lohs NEE-nyohs PAH-rah KWAHN-doh)

😄 They may also switch *niños* to *hijos*, but in both cases they are eager for you to have children.

¿Cuándo me vas a regalar un nieto? - When are you going to give me a grandchild?

(KWAHN-doh meh bahs ah rreh-gah-LAHR oon NYEH-toh)

😄 *Regalar* actually means "to gift", and though it wouldn't technically be "their" child, we know that in Latino households we are all one tightly-knit family.

Ahorita no, tía, ando enfocado/enfocada en el trabajo. - Not now, aunt, I'm focused on my work/studies.

(ah-OH-ree-tah noh TEE-ah AHN-doh ehn-foh-KAH-doh/ehn-foh-KAH-dah ehn ehl trah-BAH-hoh)

😄 We know that to *tías* our jobs are really important, so this might make her go easier on you. You could also change *trabajo* with *estudios*.

Si me los cuidas tú, ahorita mismo. - If you'll take care of them, right away.

(see meh lohs KWEE-dahs too ah-oh-REE-tah MEES-moh)

😄 This is the perfect answer to any question about having kids.

Estoy estudiando mucho. - I'm studying a lot.

(es-TOY ehs-too-dee-AHN-doh MOO-choh)

😄 Ends the topic fast, she wants you to study above all else!

Ya mero, ya mero. - Enough now.

(jah MEH-roh, jah MEH-roh)

😐 This answer is perfect to get out of any situation fast. In some countries, people may use alternatives like **Ya basta** or **Bueno, bueno**.

¿Por qué no vienes más seguido? - Why don't you come more often?
(pohr keh noh bee-EH-nehs mahs seh-GEE-doh)
😄 Another classic guilt-trip.

Lo siento, debería venir más seguido - I'm sorry, I should come more often.
(loh see-EHN-toh, de-beh-REE-ah beh-NIHR mah seh-GEE-doh)
😄 Get those puppy eyes ready to avoid being scolded further!

Congratulating the Guest of Honor

¡Felicitaciones! - Congratulations!
(feh-lee-see-tah-see-OH-nehs)
😄 Your go-to to congratulate someone for something they did.

¡Te felicito! - Congratulations!
(teh feh-lee-SEE-toh)
😄 It's a bit more personal than *felicitaciones*.

¡Feliz cumpleaños! - Happy birthday!
(feh-LEES koom-pleh-AH-nyohs)
😄 Well, you've heard this one before!

Te deseo lo mejor. - I wish you the best!
(teh de-SEH-oh loh meh-HOHR)
😄 Whether it's a birthday, a graduation, or Navidad, this is your go-to phrase after the appropriate congratulations.

Que tengas un gran día. - Have a great day!
(keh TEHN-gahs oon grahn DEE-ah)
😄 This is especially used when we're wishing someone a happy birthday.

¡Qué alegría! - How great!
(keh ah-leh-GREE-ah)
😄 *Alegría* actually means "joy".

¡Qué bueno! - How good!
(keh boo-EH-noh)
😄 Similar to ¡qué alegría! and it can be used to react to news too.

¡Me alegro por ti! - I'm happy for you!
(meh ah-LEH-groh pohr tee)
😄 We especially say this after congratulating someone for something they've achieved or done.

¡Feliz Navidad para todos! - Merry Christmas to all!
(feh-LEES nah-bee-DAHD PAH-rah TOH-dohs)
😄 Put your drink up and clink your glass with everyone else!

¡Feliz Año Nuevo, familia! - Happy New Year, family!
(feh-LEES AH-nyoh noo-EH-boh fah-MEE-lyah)
😄 *Latinos* don't really kiss on New Year's Eve, but we have other traditions, like wearing underwear of specific colors or eating grapes!

¡Felices Fiestas! - Happy Holidays!
(feh-LEE-sehs FYEHS-tahs)
😄 This one is said around Holiday-time, and it can be used to greet anyone, from family members to shopping assistants!

Feliz Día de Acción de Gracias, mamá - Happy Thanksgiving, mom!
(feh-LEES DEE-ah deh ahk-see-OHN deh GRAH-syahs mah-MAH)
😄 Though Thanksgiving isn't a *Latino* holiday, if we're in the US we may celebrate anyways!

¡Feliz Día de Gracias, abuela! - Happy Thanksgiving, grandma!
(feh-LEES DEE-ah deh GRAH-syahs, ah-BWEH-lah)

😄 We may also shorten *Día de Acción de Gracias* with just *Día de Gracias*.

¡Feliz Thanksgiving! - Happy Thanksgiving!
(feh-LEES) Thanksgiving
😄 They'll also understand if you say it in English, of course!

¡Feliz Día de Muertos! - Happy Day of the Dead!
(feh-LEES DEE-ah deh MWEHR-tohs)
😄 In Mexico, we celebrate *Día de Muertos*, and though "Happy Day of the Dead" may sound strange to us in English, it does make sense to Mexican culture.

¡Feliz día, primo! - Happy day, cousin!
(feh-LEES DEE-ah PREE-moh)
😄 This one is more general, it can be used for Christmas, a birthday or any special day or holiday.

Between Cultures: Depending on the Latin American place your family is from, they may sing *Cumpleaños feliz*, *Las mañanitas* or *Feliz cumpleaños*, which are different songs!

- In most Latino countries, people sing these lyrics to the same rhythm as the English "Happy Birthday": *Cumpleaños feliz, te deseamos a ti, cumpleaños [name], cumpleaños feliz.*

- In Mexico and other nearby countries, some people may sing "Las mañanitas": *Estas son las mañanitas que cantaba el rey David a las muchachas bonitas te las cantamos a ti.*

- In Argentina, Uruguay, and Chile, people sing these lyrics to the same rhythm as the English "Happy Birthday": *Que los cumplas feliz, que los cumplas feliz, que los cumplas [name], que los cumplas feliz.*

Getting Along

¿Quieres bailar? - Do you want to dance?
(KYEH-res bye-LAHR)
😁 Even if you can't, asking is cute.

Claro que sí. - Of course.
(KLAH-roh keh SEE)
😁 Works for any invite — food, games, shots.

Tal vez después. - Maybe later.
(tahl behs dehs-PWEHS)
😁 The polite "no thanks" for *abuela*'s dish.

Esto está delicioso. ¿Quién lo hizo? - This is delicious, who made it?
(EHS-toh ehs-TAH deh-lee-see-OH-soh kee-EHN loh EE-soh)
😁 Whoever made the dish will feel really flattered and you'll be the favorite at the party!

Cuéntame de tu vida - Tell me about your life
(koo-EHN-tah-meh deh too BEE-dah)
😁 What every Latino wants to hear in order to start talking non-stop.

¡Salud! - Cheers!
(sah-LOOD)
😁 Clink glasses with everyone.

Gossip

No lo vas a creer. - You won't believe this.
(noh loh bahs ah kreh-EHR)
😄 A great introduction to a good and juicy *chisme*. You can press your hand to your chest for added drama.

Te tengo un chisme. - I have some gossip for you.
(teh TEHN-goh oon CHEES-meh)
😄 This one's more playful, an introduction to a funnier kind of *chisme*. Place one hand on your mouth and gesture the other towards the listener in good *telenovela* style.

No sabes lo que me enteré. - You won't believe what I've heard.
(noh SAH-behs loh keh meh ehn-teh-REH)
😄 Another great introduction. We can even add pauses between each word for emphasis.

Acá entre nos, tengo algo para contarte. - Here between us, I've got something to tell you.
(ah-KAH ehn-treh nohs TEHN-goh AHL-goh PAH-rah kohn-TAHR-teh)
😄 Saying *Acá entre nos* makes it more private and secretive, a way to make them a partner in crime.

¿Sabías que...? - Did you know...?
(sah-BEE-ahs keh)
😄 This one is more direct and goes straight to telling what happened.

¿Oíste lo que sucedió? - Did you hear what happened?
(oh-EES-teh loh keh soo-seh-dee-OH)
😄 A way to introduce gossip that includes the listener.

No le puedes contar a nadie. - You can't tell anybody.
(noh leh PWEH-dehs kohn-TAHR ah NAH-dyeh)

😄 Add a serious face to let them know you mean it!

Que quede entre nosotros/nosotras. - This stays between us.
(keh KEH-de EHN-treh noh-SOH-trohs/noh-SOH-trahs)
😄 This one is less serious, and is usually accompanied by a finger twirl signaling the people involved.

Esto no puede salir de aquí, ¿eh? - This can't leave this room, ok?
(EHS-toh noh PWEH-deh sah-LEER deh ah-KEE eh)
😄 A great way to say that something is confidential.

No te lo conté yo. - You didn't hear this from me.
(noh teh loh kohn-TEH joh)
😄 Maybe *un pajarito* (a little bird) is the one who told them, but not **you**, you would never!

Cuenta, cuenta. - Pray tell.
(KWEHN-tah, KWEHN-tah)
😄 This shows our eagerness to hear the *chisme*.

No diré nada. - I won't say a thing.
(noh dih-REH NAH-dah)
😄 You can add some drama by zipping your mouth closed with your index and thumb pressed tightly together.

Soy una tumba. - My lips are sealed.
(soy OO-nah TOOM-bah)
😄 *Tumba* actually means "tomb" or "grave", it means you won't say a word!

¿Qué sucedió? - What happened?
(keh soo-seh-dee-OH)
😄 Generally asked eagerly to invite the other person to spill the beans.

¿Y qué hizo? - And what did he/she do?

(ee keh EE-soh)
😆 Asking follow-up questions shows our interest!

¿Y qué hiciste tú? - And what did you do?
(ee keh ee-SEES-teh too)
😆 If the person telling the *chisme* was involved, we need to know how they reacted!

¿Y qué pasó después? - And then what happened?
(ee keh pah-SOH dehs-PWEHS)
😆 We may show our eagerness to know with our tone or volumen—we know us Latinos can be loud.

¿En serio? - Really?
(ehn SEH-ree-oh)
😆 This is the most natural rhetorical question when we can't believe the *chisme*.

¡No puede ser! - It can't be!
(noh poo-EH-deh sehr)
😆 Press your hand to your chest for additional drama.

¡No te creo! - I can't believe it!
(noh teh KRE-oh)
😆 You can even make a dismissing gesture with your hand for emphasis.

¡No me digas! - You don't say
(noh meh DEE-gahs)
😆 You can make it as dramatic as you want by emphasizing the **digas**.

Fin de Fiesta

Adiós - Bye
(ah-dee-OHS)
🔄 In South America, instead of adiós people say **chau** or **chao**.

Gracias por invitarme - Thanks for the invitation.
(GRAH-see-ahs pohr een-bee-TAHR-meh)
😄 We always thank our relatives before leaving!

Muchas gracias por todo. - Thanks for everything.
(MOO-chahs GRAH-see-ahs pohr TOH-doh)
😄 This one's more general, but also valid and appreciated.

Estuvo increíble. - This was awesome.
(ehs-TOO-boh een-kreh-EE-bleh)
😄 If it was a *fiesta*, we should definitely add this after thanking!

La pasé genial. - I had a great time.
(lah pah-SEH heh-nee-AHL)
😄 You can say this about any gathering in general.

Espero que nos veamos pronto. - I hope we see each other again soon.
(ehs-PEH-roh keh nohs be-AH-mohs PROHN-toh)
😄 If we don't want to make any commitment, we can simply say this.

A ver cuándo repetimos. - We should do this again.
(ah behr KWAHN-doh rreh-peh-TEE-mohs)
😄 It doesn't mean you'll set a date right away, but shows you want to!

La próxima nos juntamos en mi casa. - We should do it in my house next time.
(lah PROHK-see-mah nohs hoon-TAH-mohs ehn mee KAH-sah)

😄 This is a bit more compromising, so you should invite them to your house at some point, but it definitely doesn't set this in stone.

Me voy a ir yendo. - I'll get going.
(meh BOH-ee ah eer JEHN-doh)
😄 This is what we say when we first decide to leave. It doesn't mean we'll leave right away though.

Ya me voy. - I'm leaving now. / I'm about to leave.
(jah meh BOH-ee)
😄 This can be used to say that you're leaving any minute now or to announce that you're leaving at the time.

Ya se está haciendo tarde. - It's getting late
(jah se ehs-TAH ah-see-EHN-doh TAHR-deh)
😄 The answer to your *tía*'s complaint: ¿Ya te vas? ("Are you leaving already?")

Nos vemos. - See you.
(nohs BEH-mohs)
😄 A standard goodbye.

Hasta luego. - See you later.
(AHS-tah loo-EH-goh)
😄 In some countries, this may be a bit formal.

Cuídense. - Take care.
(koo-EE-dehn-seh)
😄 This is the plural form, but if you're talking about one person only, you can say **Cuídate**.

Saluda a tu madre. - Say hi to your mom.
(sah-LOO-dah ah too MAH-dreh)
😄 This is something a member of your family or a friend of your family may say if your mom didn't attend the party, of course.

Mándales saludos a todos en casa. - Say hi to everyone at home.

(MAHN-dah-lehs sah-LOO-dohs ah TOH-dohs ehn KAH-sah)

😄 Another way to send their love to the rest of your family who couldn't come.

Vayan con cuidado. - Drive safely!

(BAH-jahn kohn kwee-DAH-doh)

😄 This is just a set phrase, there's no need to answer.

Abrígate que hace frío. - Take a coat, it's cold out!

(ah-BREE-gah-teh keh AH-seh FREE-oh)

😄 Our family will always try to take care of us! So you better put a coat on, even if it's just until you're out of view.

Avísame cuando llegues. - Let me know when you get there.

(ah-BEE-sah-meh KWAHN-doh JEH-ges)

😄 They will definitely wait for your to let them know, so shoot them a text once you're home, don't forget!

Between Cultures: This isn't exactly news, but in Latino households people say goodbye at least three times and it's a process that may take thirty minutes—if not more! First we say **Me voy a ir yendo**, which leads to a first round of *besos* and *abrazos*, but then we stay by the door talking, or your *tía* offers some food for you to take home. Once that's done, we say goodbye again near the car—this might be the place for one final *chismecito*! And then, even when we're inside the car, we keep on saying **Adiós** while making plans for next time! Make sure to plan your exit with time!

💡 No Sabo Challenge

Planning a visit to your grandma or *tía*? Record iconic parts of your visit, like the greetings, the classic *tía* phrases, their reactions to the phrases you've learned, and the classic endless Latino goodbye! Then, post your video on TikTok or Instagram with the hashtag #NoSaboChallenge! Look up the hashtag to check how other people's families are and see the similarities!

Chapter 2:

Food & Drink *Fiesta*

Food-Related Phrases

¿Puedo comer esto? - May I eat this?
(PWEH-doh koh-MEHR EHS-toh)
🍑 For when you find something yummy laying around your *tía*'s kitchen before dinner time.

Soy alérgico/alérgica al cacahuate. - I'm allergic to peanuts.
(soy ah-LEHR-hee-koh ahl kah-kah-WAH-teh)
🔄 In South America, people say *maní*.

Soy intolerante a la lactosa. - I'm lactose intolerant.
(soy een-toh-leh-RAHN-teh ah lah lahk-TOH-sah)
🍑 And we don't wanna know what happens if you eat cheese.

Soy vegetariano/vegetariana. - I'm a vegetarian.
(soy beh-heh-tah-RYAH-noh/beh-heh-tah-RYAH-nah)
🍑 Your abuela might not like it, but it's your choice.

Soy vegano/vegana. - I'm vegan.
(soy beh-GAH-noh/beh-GAH-nah)
🍑 You'll have to explain what this means to her.

No como pescado. - I don't eat fish.
(noh KOH-moh pehs-KAH-doh)
🍑 Better to let them know right away!

Tengo la presión alta. - I have high blood pressure.
(TEHN-goh lah preh-SYOHN AHL-tah)
🍑 Avoid salty food!

¿Qué trajiste? - What did you bring?
(keh trah-HEES-teh)
🍑 In Latino gatherings, it's common for everyone to bring something.

¿Esto qué tiene? - What's in this?
(EHS-toh keh TYEH-neh)
🍑 It's not rude to ask this if it's between family.

¿De qué está hecho? - What's this made of?
(deh keh ehs-TAH EH-choh)
🍑 You may ask this to find out if you can eat it or to know the ingredients because you liked it.

¿Me pasas la sal? - Can you pass the salt?
(meh PAH-sahs lah sahl)
🍑 But bear in mind that passing the salt from hand to hand is considered bad luck! Always place it on the table for the other person to grab.

¿Tienes chile? - Do you have any chili?
(TYEH-nehs CHEE-leh)
🍑 In case the food is not spicy enough.

Quiero más chile. - I want more chili.
(KYEH-roh mahs CHEE-leh)
🍑 A little more spice never hurt anybody.

Más chile, por favor. - More chili, please.
(mahs CHEE-leh pohr fah-BOHR)
🍑 Are you sure? Because maybe that's too much...

Me enchilé. - I got burned.

27

(meh ehn-chee-LEH)

🍎 I don't wanna say it but... I told you so!

Te preparo algo. - Have you eaten? I'll fix you something.

(jah koh-MEES-teh teh preh-PAH-roh AHL-goh)

🍎 No matter what time it is, you'll probably hear this the moment you step into a Latino home!

Come, que te hace falta. - Eat, you need it.

(KOH-meh keh teh HAH-seh FAHL-tah)

🍎 Again, whether you need it or not, your Latino relatives will encourage you to eat!

A la mesa, que se enfría la comida. - Come to the table, the food's getting cold.

(ah lah MEH-sah keh seh ehn-FRYAH lah koh-MEE-dah)

🍎 This is definitely in the top 5 of most heard phrases in Latino households.

Between Cultures: In the US, eating out often means fast service, large portions, and quick turnover. Waiters may bring the check without being asked. In Latin America, meals at restaurants are usually more about taking time and sharing. Service can feel slower (because the table is "yours" for the night), and it's rare to rush you out. Also, in the US, tips are 15-20%. In much of Latin America, tipping is smaller (around 10%).

At the Restaurant

Una mesa para cuatro, por favor. - A table for four, please.
(OO-nah MEH-sah PAH-rah KWAH-troh pohr fah-BOHR)
🍑 If it's a date, say *Una mesa para dos, por favor.*

Me gustaría una empanada. - I'd like an *empanada.*
(meh goos-tah-REE-ah oo-nah ehm-pah-NAH-dah)
🍑 Or change *una empanada* for *una arepa, un taco* or *un tamal.*

¿Cuál es el menú del día? - What's the dish of the day?
(kwahl ehs ehl meh-NOOH dehl DEE-ah)
🍑 It's very common for Latino restaurants to offer a starter, main course, and dessert for a fixed price.

¿Con qué acompañamiento viene el filete? - What sides come with the steak?
(kohn keh ah-kohm-pah-nyah-MYEHN-toh BYEH-neh ehl fee-LEH-TEH)
🍑 Because sometimes side dishes are even better than the main course!

¿Cuál es la pesca del día? - What's the catch of the day?
(kwahl ehs la PEHS-kah dehl dyah)
🍑 Ask this and make sure your fish is fresh.

¿Tienen cerveza en botella? - Do you have bottled beer?
(TYEH-nehn sehr-BEH-sah ehn boh-TEH-jah)
🔄 In México, it's called **chela** and it's **birra** in Argentina.

¿Puedo ver la carta de vinos? - Could I see the wine list?
(PWEH-doh behr lah KAHR-tah deh BEE-nohs)
🍑 You can use *carta de postres* for dessert and *tragos* for cocktails.

¿Este plato se puede compartir? - Is this dish shareable?
(EHS-teh PLAH-toh seh PWEH-deh kohm-pahr-TEER)

🍑 If you are not very hungry or if you think the dish might be too much for just you!

La cuenta, por favor. - The check, please.
(lah KWEHN-tah pohr fah-BOHR)
🍑 This one is from Spanish 101.

La propina no está incluida. - The tip is not included.
(lah proh-PEE-nah noh ehs-TAH een-kloo-EE-dah)
🍑 Remember that tipping varies depending on the country.

Quiero ceviche. - I want *ceviche*.
(KYEH-roh seh-BEE-cheh)
✏️ *Quiero* is your best friend—just use it followed by whatever it is you want to order!

¿Qué hay? - What do you have?
(keh AH-y)
🍑 This way, you can hear the server say the dishes and then just copy the pronunciation!

¿Qué recomiendas? - What do you recommend?
(keh rreh-koh-MYEHN-dahs)
🍑 This is another way to avoid having to read out loud in Spanish. Just trust your server!

¡Qué lo disfruten! - Enjoy!
(keh loh dees-FROO-tehn)
🍑 You'll probably hear this from your server after they've brought your order.

After Eating

¡Qué rico! - How good!
(keh RREE-koh)
🍑 Say this to you *abuela* after eating her food and she'll love you.

¡Qué delicia! - How tasty!
(keh deh-LEE-syah)
🍑 Another good phrase to compliment your relative's food.

¿Cómo está? - How is it?
(KOH-moh ehs-TAH)
🍑 Whoever cooked will want to know this as soon as you are done—or even before!

Estuvo riquísimo. - It was exquisite.
(ehs-TOO-boh rree-KEE-see-moh)
🍑 You can answer this if you loved the meal (or if you don't want to offend anyone).

Está picante. - It's spicy.
(ehs-TAH pee-KAHN-teh)
🍑 Say this when your *abuela* went to far with the chili.

Está un poco soso. - It's a bit bland.
(ehs-TAH oon POH-koh SOH-soh)
🍑 You can say this or just ask for some salt.

Todo estuvo exquisito. - Everything was exquisite.
(TOH-doh ehs-TOO-boh eks-kee-SEE-toh)
🍑 A great way to compliment the chef.

Me encantó todo. - I loved everything.
(meh ehn-kahn-TOH TOH-doh)
🍑 Another nice compliment.

¿Te gustó? - Did you like it?
(teh goos-TOH)
🍎 You'll probably hear this at some point during the meal. Your answer has to be *sí*.

¿Quieres más? - Do you want more?
(KYEH-rehs mahs)
🍎 And you'll DEFINITELY hear this as soon as you are done.

¿Quieres repetir? - Do you want seconds?
(KYEH-rehs rreh-peh-TEER)
🍎 In the same line as the question above. Don't you dare say no.

¿Por qué no comes más, no te gustó? - Why don't you eat more, you didn't like it?
(pohr keh noh KOH-mehs mahs noh teh goos-TOH)
🍎 For some reason, Latino people associate eating a normal portion with not liking the food.

Ya estoy lleno/llena, gracias. - I'm full, thanks.
(jah ehs-TOY JEH-noh/JEH-nah GRAH-syahs)
🍎 You can always decline with this polite answer.

Llévate un poco. - Take some.
(JEH-bah-teh oon POH-koh)
🍎 But you'll probably end up taking leftovers home.

💡 No Sabo Challenge

Pick a simple family recipe (like *tacos*, *arroz con pollo* or *empanadas*) and record yourself cooking it while saying every ingredient and step in Spanish. Don't worry if your Spanish isn't perfect—that's the fun part! Then, ask a family member or friend to try the dish and capture their reaction. Post your video on TikTok or Instagram with the hashtag #NoSaboChallenge, and see how others are sharing their *comida* traditions!

Chapter 3:

Flirting & Dating *en Español*

First Impressions

¿Eres de por aquí? - Are you from around here?
(EH-rehs deh pohr ah-KEE)
🔄 In countries that use *vos*, the question would be ¿Sos de por acá?

¿Qué te trae por aquí? - What brings you here?
(keh teh TRAH-eh pohr ah-KEE)
🌹 A good question to avoid a simple "yes" or "no" answer.

¿Has venido con alguien? - Are you here with someone?
(ahs beh-NEE-doh kohn AHL-gyehn)
🌹 A way of knowing if they came alone or not.

¿Te invito un trago? - Can I buy you a drink?
(teh een-BEE-toh oon TRAH-goh)
💘 A drink might help with your nerves.

¿Qué tomas? - What are you drinking?
(keh TOH-mahs)
💘 A variation with more confidence.

Getting to Know Each Other

¿Cómo te llamas? - What's your name?
(KOH-moh teh JAH-mahs)
💘 The bare minimum.

¿Cómo es tu nombre? - What's your name?
(KOH-moh ehs too NOHM-breh)
💘 A common variation.

¿Cuántos años tienes? - How old are you?
(KWAHN-tohs AH-nyohs TYEH-nehs)
💘 Would you date some older or younger than you?

¿A qué te dedicas? - What do you do?
(ah keh teh deh-DEE-kahs)
💘 Someone who works and/or studies is usually a good catch.

¿De qué trabajas? - What's your job?
(deh keh trah-BAH-hahs)
💘 It doesn't matter how much they make!

¿De dónde eres? - Where are you from?
(deh DOHN-deh EH-rehs)
💘 Multicultural love is a great experience.

¿Qué haces en tu tiempo libre? - What do you do in your free time?
(keh AH-sehs ehn too TYEHM-poh LEE-breh)
💕 Hobbies can bring people closer.

¿Tienes algún pasatiempo? - Do you have any hobbies?
(TYEH-nehs ahl-GOON pah-sah-TYEHM-poh)
💕 A possible variation.

¿Haces algún deporte? - Do you practice any sports?
(AH-sehs ahl-GOON deh-POHR-teh)
💕 A sound mind in a sound body.

Asking Someone Out

¿Tienes pareja? - Do you have a partner?
(TYEH-nehs pah-REH-hah)
🖊 *Pareja* works for both men and women.

¿Estás de novio/novia? - Do you have a boyfriend/girlfriend?
(ehs-TAHS deh NOH-byoh/NOH-byah)
💕 An important piece of information if you want to date someone.

¿Me darías tu número? - Would you give me your number?
(meh dah-REE-ahs too NOO-meh-roh)
💕 You can text them later.

¿Tienes planes para este fin de semana? - Do you have plans for the weekend?
(TYEH-nehs PLAH-nehs PAH-rah EHS-teh feen deh seh-MAH-nah)
💕 Weekends are great for dates!

¿Haces algo el viernes próximo? - Are you doing anything

next Friday?
(AH-sehs AHL-goh ehl BYEHR-nehs PROHK-see-moh)
💘 Who isn't free Friday?

¿Te gustaría salir alguna vez? - Would you like to go out some time?
(teh goos-tah-REE-ah sah-LEER ahl-GOO-nah behs)
💘 Simple and direct.

¿Vamos al cine? - Do you want to go to the movies?
(BAH-mohs ahl SEE-neh)
💘 The movie will do the talking for you.

¿Quieres venir a una fiesta? - Do you want to come to a party?
(KYEH-rehs beh-NEER ah OO-nah FYEHS-tah)
💘 Win them over with your dance moves!

Catcalling

¿Crees en el amor a primera vista o vuelvo a pasar? - Do you believe in love at first sight or should I walk past you again?
(KREH-ehs ehn ehl ah-MOHR ah pree-MEH-rah BEEHS-tah oh BWEHL-boh ah pah-SAHR)
💘 Have you ever fallen in love at first sight?

No eres Google, pero tienes todo lo que busco. - You're not Google, but you have everything I'm searching for.
(noh EH-rehs GOO-gle PEH-roh TYEH-nehs TOH-doh loh keh BOOS-koh)
💘 You have all the answers.

Se te cayó un papel... El que te envuelve, bombón - You dropped your wrapper... bonbon.
(seh teh kah-JOH oon pah-PEHL... ehl keh teh ehn-BWEHL-

36

beh bohm-BOHN)
💘 Win them over with your dance moves!

Quisiera ser la tortilla de tu taco - You are the tortilla to my taco.
(kee-SYEH-rah sehr lah tohr-TEE-yah theh too TAH-koh)
🔄 In Argentina, there's a variation that goes ***Soy el puré de tu milanesa*** ("I'm the mash potatoes to your breaded cutlet").

En esa cola sí me formo - I'll be sure get in that line.
(ehn EH-sah KOH-lah see meh FOHR-moh)
✏️ *Cola* means both "line" and "booty" in Spanish.

¿De qué juguetería te escapaste, muñeca? - What toy store did you run away from, doll?
(deh keh hoo-geh-teh-REE-ah teh ehs-kah-PAHS-teh moo-NYEH-kah)
💘 Did you like playing with dolls?

Between Cultures: Keep in mind that catcalling can be considered offensive, especially if it's done to random people on the street. You can use these phrases jokingly with someone with whom you have mutual trust.

Before Leaving

Fue un gusto conocerte. - It was a pleasure to meet you.
(fweh oon GOOS-toh koh-noh-SEHR-teh)
💕 A lovely way of ending a date.

Encantado/Encantada de conocerte. - Enchanted to meet you.
(ehn-kahn-TAH-doh/ehn-kahn-TAH-dah deh koh-noh-SEHR-teh)
💕 A more affectionate variation.

Me gustaría verte de nuevo. - I'd like to see you again.
(meh goos-tah-REE-ah BEHR-teh deh NWEH-boh)
💕 Don't let the opportunity pass you by!

¿Te gustaría volver a vernos? - Would you like to see each other again?
(teh goos-tah-REE-ah bohl-BEHR ah BEHR-nohs)
💕 A less direct variation.

Me encantó hablar contigo. - I loved talking to you.
(meh ehn-kahn-TOH ah-BLAHR kohn-TEE-goh)
💕 Deep conversations lead to strong connections.

Breaking Up

Tenemos que hablar... - We have to talk...
(teh-NEH-mohs keh ah-BLAHR)
💘 Uh-oh.

Creo que esto no funciona. - I think this isn't working.
(KREH-oh keh EHS-toh noh foon-SYOH-nah)
💘 My heart just stopped.

Necesito espacio. - I need some space.
(neh-seh-SEE-toh ehs-PAH-syoh)
💘 Holding back tears at this point..

Tomémonos un tiempo. - Let's take a break.
(toh-MEH-moh-nohs oon TYEHM-poh)
💘 We're never seeing each other again.

No estamos en la misma sintonía. - We're not in sync.
(noh ehs-TAH-mohs ehn lah MEES-mah seen-toh-NEE-ah)
💘 Here come the waterworks.

Ya no siento lo mismo. - I don't feel the same way anymore.
(yah noh SYEHN-toh loh MEES-moh)
💘 Nothing's like before.

Es mejor que terminemos. - It's better if we break up.
(ehs meh-HOHR keh tehr-mee-NEH-mohs)
💘 It's over.

No quiero lastimarte, pero... - I don't want to hurt you, but...
(noh KYEH-roh lahs-tee-MAHR-teh PEH-roh)
💘 You already did.

Creo que es momento de decir adiós. - I think it's time to say goodbye.

(KREH-oh keh ehs moh-MEHN-toh deh deh-SEER ah-DYOHS)
💔 I can't.

Somos muy distintos. - We're very different.
(SOH-mohs mooy dees-TEEN-tohs)
💔 But that's what I like about you!

No eres tú, soy yo. - It's not you, it's me.
(noh EH-rehs too soy joh)
💔 An all-time classic.

Ojalá podamos seguir siendo amigos. - I hope we can still be friends.
(oh-hah-LAH poh-DAH-mohs seh-GEER SYEHN-doh ah-MEE-gohs)
💔 Not the friendzone!

Te veo más como amigo/amiga. - I see you more as a friend.
(teh BEH-oh mahs KOH-moh ah-MEE-goh/ah-MEE-gah)
💔 An alternative that still hurts.

No estoy para algo serio. - I'm not looking for anything serious.
(noh ehs-TOY PAH-rah AHL-goh SEH-ryoh)
💔 I see.

No tenemos tiempo el uno para el otro. - We don't have time for each other.
(noh teh-NEH-mohs TYEHM-poh ehl OO-noh PAH-rah ehl OH-troh)
💔 That won't work.

Necesito enfocarme en mí mismo/misma. - I need to focus on myself.
(neh-seh-SEE-toh ehn-foh-KAHR-meh ehn mee MEES-moh/MEES-mah)
💔 I understand...

Necesito tiempo para mí. - I need time for myself.
(neh-seh-SEE-toh TYEHM-poh PAH-rah mee)
💢 A sad alternative.

Dejemos de hablar por un tiempo. - Let's not talk for a while.
(deh-HEH-mohs deh ah-BLAHR pohr oon TYEHM-poh)
💢 For how long?

Espero que encuentres a alguien mejor. - I hope you find someone better.
(ehs-PEH-roh keh ehn-KWEHN-trehs ah AHL-gyehn meh-HOHR)
💢 I hope so, too.

Todavía me duele, pero estoy bien. - It still hurts, but I'm okay.
(toh-dah-BEE-ah meh DWEH-leh PEH-roh ehs-TOY byehn)
💢 Healing takes time.

Borré sus mensajes. - I deleted their texts.
(boh-RREH soos mehn-SAH-hehs)
💢 It hurts too much.

Me bloqueó en redes sociales. - They blocked me on social media.
(meh bloh-KEOH ehn RREH-dehs soh-SYAH-lehs)
💢 I don't want to see their face.

Me rompió el corazón. - They broke my heart.
(meh rrohm-PYOH ehl koh-rah-SOHN)
💢 Ouch!

¡Me engañó! - They cheated on me!
(meh ehn-gah-NYOH)
🔵 Other variants include ***Me metió los cuernos*** or ***Me puso***

los cachos (literally: "They stuck their horns into me").

Me dejó por otra persona. - They left me for someone else.
(meh deh-HOH pohr OH-trah pehr-SOH-nah)
💘 Oh no!

Lo/La dejé. - I left him/her.
(loh/lah deh-HEH)
💘 Finally!

Ya no estaba enamorado/enamorada. - I wasn't in love anymore.
(jah noh ehs-TAH-bah eh-nah-moh-RAH-doh/eh-nah-moh-RAH-dah)
💘 Then it was time to leave.

Es mejor así. - It's better this way.
(ehs meh-HOHR ah-SEE)
💘 That's right.

💡 No Sabo Challenge

Want to pick up a girl or guy in Spanish? Record a night out as you try your luck with some of the phrases you've learned. Who knows? Maybe you get a phone number or two. If you're already in a relationship, you can use these phrases with your SO to see their reaction. Then, post your video on TikTok or Instagram (with the person's permission, of course) with the hashtag #NoSaboChallenge! Look up the hashtag to check how others have done.

Chapter 4:

Everyday Life Quick Wins

Morning

Me despierto a las siete y media. - I wake up at seven thirty.
(meh dehs-PYEHR-toh ah lahs SYEH-teh ee MEH-dyah)
🕐 The early bird catches the worm!

Me levanto de la cama. - I get out of bed.
(meh leh-BAHN-toh deh lah KAH-mah)
🕐 Remember to get out *con el pie derecho.*

Me ducho por las mañanas. - I shower in the mornings.
(meh DOO-choh pohr lahs mah-NYAH-nahs)
🕐 Some people shower in the morning and some people do it at night.

Me lavo los dientes. - I brush my teeth.
(meh LAH-boh lohs DYEHN-tehs)
🔄 You can also say ***me cepillo*** *los dientes.*

Me afeito cada mañana. - I shave every morning.
(meh ah-FEHY-toh KAH-dah mah-NYAH-nah)
🕐 Whether you shave or not, you should know this verb.

Me maquillo un poco. - I put on a little makeup.
(meh mah-KEE-joh oon POH-koh)
🕐 A little *lápiz labial* (lipstick) never hurt anyone.

Preparo café. - I make coffee.
(preh-PAH-roh kah-FEH)
🕐 You can't call yourself Latino if you don't like coffee!

Desayuno pan con huevo. - I have bread with egg for breakfast.
(deh-sah-JOO-noh pahn kohn WEH-boh)
🕐 A healthy *desayuno* to start the day!

Leo las noticias. - I read the news.
(LEH-oh lahs noh-TEE-syahs)
🕐 You can also say ***Leo el diario*** ("I read the newspaper").

Salgo de casa a las ocho. - I leave home at eight.
(SAHL-goh deh KAH-sah ah lahs OH-choh)
🕐 Do you work during the day or the night?

Between Cultures: In the US, people often wake up before sunrise, start work around 8 a.m., have lunch at noon, dinner around 6 p.m., and are in bed by 10. In much of Latin America, the day starts later and is more flexible. Dinner can be as late as 9 or 10 p.m., and social life often stretches past midnight. They have a *merienda* (an afternoon snack) between lunch and dinner! Even work and school schedules tend to start a bit later compared to the US.

Afternoon

Voy al trabajo en autobús. - I take the bus to work.
(bohy ahl trah-BAH-joh ehn ah-oo-toh-BOOS)
🕐 Although *autobús* is widely recognized in Latin America, there are many other words to refer to this universal mode of transport, including **micro**, **colectivo**, **bus**, and **guagua**. If you use *bus*, be aware of the Spanish pronunciation!

Almuerzo en mi escritorio. - I have lunch at my desk.
(ahl-MWEHR-soh ehn mee ehs-kree-TOH-ryoh)
🕐 Although we hope you don't have lunch at your desk.

Voy al gimnasio por la tarde. - I go to the gym in the afternoon.
(bohy ahl heem-NAH-syoh pohr lah TAHR-deh)
🕐 Good for you!

Hago la compra. - I go grocery shopping.
(AH-goh lah KOHM-prah)
🕐 Who's in charge of groceries in your household?

Busco a los niños por la escuela. - I pick up the kids from school.
(BOOS-koh ah lohs NEE-nyohs pohr lah ehs-KWEH-lah)

🕐 Don't you forget this task!

Evening

Vuelvo a casa a las seis. - I come back home at six.
(BWEL-boh ah KAH-sah ah lahs sehys)
🕐 Six ain't that bad, is it?

Preparo la cena. - I make dinner.
(preh-PAH-roh lah SEH-nah)
🕐 Some tacos, maybe?

Me acuesto en la cama. - I lie down in bed.
(meh ah-KWEHS-toh ehn lah KAH-mah)
🕐 Finally, the day is over!

Me duermo temprano. - I go to sleep early.
(meh DWEHR-moh tehm-PRAH-noh)
🕐 *Mañana será otro día* (tomorrow will be another day!).

💡 **No Sabo Challenge**

Put everything you've learned in this chapter into practice! Film a short vlog of your day, but narrate every action in Spanish as you do it. Use at least five phrases from today's lesson, but adapt them to your timetable and activities. Post your video on TikTok or Instagram with the hashtag #NoSaboChallenge and check out how other people show their everyday routines in Spanish!

Chapter 5:

Shopping & Money

General Shopping

¿En qué puedo ayudarte? - What can I help you with?
(ehn keh PWEH-doh ah-joo-DAHR-teh)
🛍️ This is what a sales clerk will most likely say to you first. It may be right when you enter the store or a bit later.

¿Buscas algo? - Are you looking for something?
(BOOS-kahs AHL-goh)
🛍️ This is another question they may ask you while you're browsing.

Solo estoy mirando. - I'm just looking.
(SOH-loh ehs-TOY mee-RAHN-doh)
🛍️ Sometimes its ok if you're just up for browsing..

Estoy buscando una mochila. - I'm looking for a backpack.
(ehs-TOY boos-KAHN-doh OO-nah moh-CHEE-lah)
🛍️ Practice being as specific as you can, even if you need to use lots of words to describe an object.

¿Es para regalo? - Is it a gift?
(ehs PAH-rah rreh-GAH-loh)
🛍️ It's always a nice gesture to take home some souvenirs for friends and family. .

¿Quieres una bolsa? - Do you want a bag?

(KYEH-rehs OO-nah BOHL-sah)

🛒 In some places, there is an extra charge for paper or plastic bags, so they may ask if you want one instead of just giving you one.

> **Between Cultures:** You know "Secret Santa", right? Well, in Latin America we have *amigo secreto* ("secret friend"), *amigo invisible* ("invisible friend") or even *angelito* ("little angel"), and it isn't for Christmas necessarily. The game mechanics are the same—everyone is assigned a gift recipient for a particular date. It is common during *Navidad* with friends or family, but it is also common in other Latin American countries like Colombia, Paraguay and Argentina, for dates dedicated exclusively to friendship: *Día del Amor y la Amistad*, *Día de la Amistad*, or *Día del Amigo*. When you play *amigo secreto*, in some countries you even leave clues the days before the grand reveal, so the person can start guessing who it is.

Paying

Fue costoso. - It was expensive.
(fweh kohs-TOH-soh)
🛒 This is an standard way of saying this, you can say *carísimo* instead of *costoso* if you want to emphasize it and make it more colloquial.

Fue una ganga. - It was a steal.
(fweh OO-nah GAHN-gah)
🛒 This is a colloquial way to say it was cheap, the more standard way would be *Salió barato*.

Vale la pena. - It's worth it.
(BAH-leh lah PEH-nah)
🛒 Use it when something looks pricey but you want to sound

like a wise *abuela*: "It's worth it, *m'ijo*."

Cuesta un ojo de la cara. - It costs an arm and a leg.
(KWEHS-tah oon OH-hoh deh lah KAH-rah)
📱 Latino way to say "that's crazy expensive." Don't worry, you get to keep both eyes. ••

¿Cuánto cuesta? - How much is it?
(KWAHN-toh KWEHS-tah)
📱 The universal phrase. Even if you only know this, you can survive any *tiendita*.

¿Me haces un descuento? - Can you offer a discount?
(meh AH-sehs oon dehs-KWEHN-toh)
📱 Channel your inner *tía* at the flea market—some *Latinos* always ask for a discount, it's tradition.

Hay 2×1 en el cine. - There's 2 for 1 at the movies.
(AH-y dohs pohr OO-noh ehn ehl SEE-neh)
📱 Best excuse to shoot your shot: "Come with me, it's basically free." 🎬

Te hago una transferencia. - I'll make a bank transfer/I'll wire you the money.
(teh AH-goh OO-nah trahns-feh-REHN-syah)
📱 Fancy way to pay in most places, but common in Argentina.

Mándame el dinero por Zelle. - Send me the money via Zelle.
(MAHN-dah-meh ehl dee-NEH-roh pohr) Zelle
📱 If you're in the US, this phrase = survival. Everyone's on Zelle.

Te lo envío por Venmo. - I'll Venmo you
(teh loh ehn-BEE-oh pohr) Venmo
📱 College kids' favorite. Perfect for splitting tacos 🌮 or Uber rides.

¿Aceptas pago con QR? - Do you accept QR payment?
(ah-SEHP-tahs PAH-goh kohn KUH-erre)
🏧 Whip out your phone and boom, paid.

Mándame tu cuenta de PayPal. - Send me you PayPal
account.
(MAHN-dah-meh too KWEHN-tah deh) PayPal
🏧 Old school but global. Works for *tías* in México AND
cousins in Chile.

¿Puedo pagar con crédito? - Can I pay with credit card?
(PWEH-doh PAH-gahr kohn KREH-dee-toh)
🏧 Smooth way to ask if your plastic money works here. 💳

¿Tienes cambio de 100? - Do you have change for 100?
(TYEH-nehs KAHM-byoh deh syehn)
🏧 Taxi drivers' worst nightmare, but necessary.

¿Hay descuento en efectivo? - Is there a cash discount?
(AH-y dehs-KWEHN-toh ehn eh-fehk-TEE-boh)
🏧 Latino life hack: cash = usually cheaper. Your wallet will
thank you.

No llevo efectivo. - I don't have cash on me.
(noh JEH-boh eh-fehk-TEE-boh)
🏧 The perfect excuse when your *primo* asks you to cover the
bill. 😅

Shopping for Clothes

¿Lo tienes en otro color? - Do you have this in another color?
(loh TYEH-nehs ehn OH-troh koh-LOHR)
🏧 Swap color for *talla* or *modelo* to sound extra practical:
¿Lo tienes en otra talla?

¿Me lo puedo probar? - Can I try it on?
(meh loh PWEH-doh proh-BAHR)
🔄 You can switch probar for medir in some places (mainly *México*): ¿Me lo puedo medir?

¿Tienes una talla más grande? - Do you have a bigger size?
(TYEH-nehs OO-nah TAH-jah mahs GRAHN-deh)
🛍️ You can also change *grande* with **chica** to ask for a smaller size.

¡Te queda increíble! - It looks great on you!
(teh KEH-dah een-kreh-EE-bleh)
🛍️ You can also say ¡Te queda perfecto! for the same hype effect.

¿Cómo me queda? - How does it look?
(KOH-moh meh KEH-dah)
🛍️ Alternative: ¿Se me ve bien?

Ese color te sienta muy bien. - That color looks good on you.
(EH-seh koh-LOHR teh SYEHN-tah mooy byehn)
🛍️ That yellow shirt *te queda perfecto*.

Me queda un poco chico. - It's a bit small.
(meh KEH-dah oon POH-koh CHEE-koh)
🛍️ You can replace *chico* with **grande** as you see fit.

Me gusta más en blanco. - I like it better in white.
(meh GOOS-tah mahs ehn BLAHN-koh)
🛍️ You can switch *blanco* for any other color you like.

¿Dónde está el probador? - Where is the changing room?
(DOHN-deh ehs-TAH ehl proh-bah-DOHR)
🔄 In México you'll hear **vestidor**, in Argentina **probador** — same concept.

Combina muy bien con tu falda roja. - It matches great with

your red skirt.
(kohn-BEE-nah mooy BYEHN kohn too FAHL-dah RROH-hah)
🛍️ Replace *falda roja* with any clothing item: *con tu camisa negra, con esos zapatos.*

Te queda pintado. - It looks great on you.
(teh KEH-dah peen-TAH-doh)
🔄 A phrase mainly used by Argentinian or Uruguayan *abuelas*, but you can also say **Te queda al centavo** in Mexico, **Te queda brutal** in Caribbean countries or **Te queda chévere** in many other countries, like Venezuela, Peru, and Mexico.

¿Es muy formal? - Is it too formal?
(ehs mooy fohr-MAHL)
🛍️ You can swap *formal* for **informal** or **casual** depending on the vibe.

Me gusta el que tiene rayas. - I like the striped one.
(meh goos-tah ehl keh TYEH-neh RRAH-jahs)
🛍️ Change *rayas* to **cuadros** (plaid) or **lunares** (polka dots). Handy shopping vocab.

Money Talk

No tengo un peso. - I don't have a dime.
(noh TEHN-goh oon PEH-soh)
🔄 Swap *peso* for any currency: **No tengo un dólar**, **No tengo un sol**.

Ando corto de lana. - I'm short on cash.
(AHN-doh KOHR-toh deh LAH-nah)
🔄 In México: *lana* = cash. In Argentina: **guita**. In Puerto Rico: **chavos**.

Estoy en la quiebra. - I'm broke.

(ehs-TOY ehn lah KYEH-brah)

💰 If you say this you aren't literally broke, but **en cero**, with no money, at least until the next paycheck.

Paga lo que debes. - Pay what you owe.
(PAH-gah loh keh DEH-behs)

💰 You can flip debes → me debes for a direct roast: "Pay me, bro."

Me toca invitar. - It's my turn to treat you.
(meh TOH-kah een-bee-TAHR)

💰 Though *invitar* means "to invite", it implies that you're paying! So be careful how you use *invitar*.

Hagamos una vaquita. - Let's all chip in.
(ah-GAH-mohs OO-nah bah-KEE-tah)

💰 It is used in many places to gather money for a particular cause or to gift to someone.

Nos toca apretar el cinturón. - It's time to tighten the belt
(nohs TOH-kah ah-preh-TAHR ehl seen-too-ROHN)

💰 You might also hear **hay que ahorrar** (we have to save) which is less figurative.

El dinero atrae más dinero. - Money attracts more money.
(ehl dee-NEH-roh ah-TRAH-eh mahs dee-NEH-roh)

💰 A set phrase you might hear you *abuela* say.

El dinero no crece de los árboles. - Money doesn't grow from trees.
(ehl dee-NEH-roh noh KREH-seh deh lohs AHR-boh-lehs)

💰 In South American countries, like Argentina, Uruguay and Chile, you might hear **plata**, but in others, they will definitely say *dinero*.

El que no arriesga, no gana. - You have to be in it to win it.

(ehl keh noh ah-RRYEHS-gah noh GAH-nah)
🏦 This is usually used to talk about *apuestas* (betting), or it could be about investments if you're a cryptobro.

¿Cuánto pagas de renta? - How much rent do you pay?
(KWAHN-toh PAH-gas deh RREHN-tah)
🏦 Depending on where you are, you might hear **alquiler** instead of *renta*.

Tengo que pagar la hipoteca. - I have to pay my mortgage.
(TEHN-goh keh pah-GAHR lah ee-poh-TEH-kah)
🏦 Adulting level unlocked. 😭

Pedí un préstamo en el banco. - I asked for a loan at the bank.
(peh-DEE oon PREHS-tah-moh ehn ehl BAHN-koh)
🏦 Also works with *crédito* (credit): **Pedí un crédito en el banco**.

Odio llevar monedas. - I hate carrying coins.
(OH-dyoh JEH-bahr moh-NEH-dahs)

🏰 And, in some Latin countries, they aren't even worth much.

💡 No Sabo Challenge

Let your *tía*, *mamá*, *abuela*, *primo*—or anybody, really—take you shopping in their home country or around a *Latino* neighborhood. Ask them to take you to their favorite places and record your trip. Remember to *saludar* the shop clerks, use the phrases in this chapter and, if your relative is a regular with the shop owners, why not strike up a conversation and explain what you're doing there? To end the day trip, treat your relative to something to eat, and you handle the full transaction! Tell them that *es tu turno de invitar* and ask the seller how you can pay. Once the video is ready, upload it to TikTok or Instagram with the hashtag #NoSaboChallenge to see how others handled and the reaction in their *abuela*'s faces when they treat them!

Chapter 6:

Sin Pena Confidence Boosters

Latino origins

Mis padres son mexicanos. - My parents are Mexican.
(mees PAH-drehs sohn meh-hee-KAH-nohs)
🌍 Did you know that Mexico has the largest Spanish-speaking population in the world?

Mi abuela es de Cuba. - My grandma is from Cuba.
(mee ah-BWEH-lah ehs deh KOO-bah)
🌍 *Abuela* stories are always the best. If you have an *abuela*, ask her to tell you about her youth.

No soy boricua, soy tico. - I'm not *Boricua*, I'm *Tico*.
(noh soy boh-REE-kwah, soy TEE-koh)
🌍 *Boricua* = Puerto Rican, *Tico* = Costa Rican. Wear your identity with pride!

¿Eres chicana también? - Are you Chicana too?
(EH-rehs chee-KAH-nah tahm-BYEHN)
🌍 *Chicana/o* is a proud identity for many Mexican-Americans.

¿De dónde eres? - Where are you from?
(deh DOHN-deh EH-rehs)
🌍 One of the first questions you'll hear in Spanish—be ready to answer!

¿Dónde naciste? - Where were you born?
(DOHN-deh nah-SEES-teh)
🌍 A variation of the previous one.

¿De dónde son tus padres? - Where are your parents from?
(deh DOHN-deh sohn toos PAH-drehs)
🌍 This question gets you straight into family history.

¿Cuál es tu ascendencia? - What's your ancestry?
(kwahl ehs too ah-sehn-DEN-syah)
🌍 A more formal way of asking about your roots.

Mi familia llegó en 1960. - My family arrived in 1960.
(mee fah-MEE-lyah jeh-GOH ehn meehl noh-beh-SYEHN-tohs seh-SEHN-tah)
🔄 You can also say the short version *Mil nueve sesenta*.

Mi madre quería un futuro mejor para nosotros. - My mother wanted a better future for us.
(mee MAH-dreh keh-REE-ah oon foo-TOO-roh meh-HOHR PAH-rah noh-SOH-trohs)
🌍 A classic immigrant family story.

Phrases About your Spanish

¡Qué bien hablas español! - You speak Spanish so well!
(keh byehn AH-blahs ehs-pah-NYOHL)
🌍 Always take this compliment, even if you don't believe it's true.

Estoy aprendiendo español. - I'm learning Spanish.
(ehs-TOY ah-prehn-DYEHN-doh ehs-pah-NYOHL)
🌍 A humble and honest statement—people love it.

Sé hablar un poco de español. - I can speak a little Spanish.

(seh ah-BLAHR oon POH-koh deh ehs-pah-NYOHL)
🌎 *Un poco* is enough to make a lot of friends!

Mi español no es muy bueno. - My Spanish is not very good.
(mee ehs-pah-NYOHL noh ehs mooy BWEH-noh)
🌎 Don't worry—bad Spanish is better than no Spanish.

¿Puedes repetir, por favor? - Can you repeat, please?
(PWEH-dehs reh-peh-TEER por fah-BOHR)
🌎 Magic phrase for learners. Use it without shame!

¿Qué dijiste? - What did you say?
(keh dee-HEES-teh)
🌎 Short, direct, and super useful.

¿Puedes hablar más despacio? -Can you
speak more slowly?
(PWEH-dehs ah-BLAHR mahs dehs-PAH-syoh)
🌎 Essential for survival—no lerner understands fast speech.

Perdón, no te oí. - Sorry, I didn't hear you.
(pehr-DOHN noh teh oh-EE)
🌎 Blame your ears, not your Spanish.

No te entiendo bien. - I can't understand you well.
(noh teh ehn-TYEHN-doh byehn)
🌎 Most people will happily rephrase.

Between Cultures: It's normal for native speakers to mock your Spanish, but don't be discouraged! They're doing it from a place of love and they'll be delighted to know you're trying to improve your Spanish.

💡 No Sabo Challenge

Ask your parents, grandparents, or any relative about your family's roots. Use the following questions: ¿De dónde eres? ¿De dónde son tus padres? ¿Dónde naciste? Record a short video introducing yourself in Spanish with pride. For example: *Hola, me llamo* [your name]. *Mis padres son* [their nationality]. *Mi familia llegó en* [year]. *Estoy aprendiendo español.*" Post your video on TikTok or Instagram with the hashtag #NoSaboChallenge, and check how other people proudly share their family stories!

Chapter 7:

Pop Culture & TikTok *en Español*

Telenovela Culture

¡Ay, Dios mío! - Oh, my God!
(ahy dyohs MEE-oh)
📺 A typical soap opera phrase used for dramatization; today it's used to express surprise or shock.

¡Oh, por Dios! - Oh, my God!
(oh pohr dyohs)
📺 It is used the same as in English, with an ironic or exaggerated tone. The *oh* part is probably copied from the Spanish dubbing of English movies.

Con todo respeto, Doctor, pero qué chismoso. - With all due respect, Doctor, but you're so nosy.
(kohn TOH-doh rehs-PEH-toh DOHK-tor PEH-roh keh chees-MOH-soh)
📺 This one comes from *Yo soy Betty, la fea* (or *Betty, la fea*, for short), a famous Colombian *telenovela*. It's used to accuse someone of being nosy. You can say it to your *tía* if she's asking too many questions!

¡Betty, me llevan! - Betty, they're taking me away!
(BEH-tee meh JEH-bahn)
📺 Another one from the great *Betty, la fea*—which we highly recommend, by the way. This one is used to exaggerate panic or nervousness.

La pobreza me está respirando aquí en la nuca, Marce. - Poverty is breathing down my neck, Marce.
(lah poh-BREH-sah meh ehs-TAH rehs-pee-RAHN-doh ah-KEE ehn lah NOO-kah MAHR-seh)
📺 This classic from the Colombian *telenovela* fills social media when the end of the month approaches.

Perdóname pero discúlpame. - Forgive me but excuse me.
(pehr-DOH-nah-meh PEH-roh dees-KOOL-pah-meh)
📺 This redundant apology was made popular by Freddy Steward, a secondary character in *Betty, la fea*.

¡Y llegaron los meseros! - And the waiters arrived!
(ee jeh-GAH-rohn lohs meh-SEH-rohs)
📺 The last one brought to us by Betty. This one is used to describe chaotic, unexpected or intense situations.

Maldita lisiada. - Damned crippled woman.
(mal-DEE-tah lee-SYAH-dah)
📺 From *María la del barrio*, a famous Mexican soap opera. Today it's a worldwide meme used to mock melodrama.

Fue sin querer queriendo. - It was accidentally on purpose.
(fweh seen keh-REHR keh-RYEHN-doh)
📺 Made popular by the endearing main character of the Mexican sitcom *El chavo del 8*.

¡Eso, eso, eso! - Yes, yes, yes!
(HE-soh HE-soh HE-soh)
📺 El Chavo used to exclaim this phrase for an emphatic yes, and he accompanied it with the hand gesture Mexicans use to affirm.

¡Que no panda el cúnico! - Don't panic!
(keh noh KOON-dah ehl PAH-nee-koh)
📺 *El Chapulín Colorado*, Mexico's superhero, used to mixed up idioms and letters. This phrase is a spoonerism of the correct *Que no cunda el pánico*.

¿Usted sabe quién soy yo? - Do you know who I am?
(oos-TEHD SAH-beh kyehn soy joh)
📺 Typical of arrogant characters; used to mock someone with airs of grandeur.

Reggaeton Culture

Las mujeres ya no lloran, las mujeres facturan. - Women don't cry anymore, women cash in.
(lahs moo-HEH-rehs jah noh JOH-rahn, lahs moo-HEH-rehs fahk-TOO-rahn)
📺 From Shakira's breakup song; used as a women empowering slogan.

¿A quién le importa lo que yo haga? - Who cares what I do?
(ah kyehn leh eem-POHR-tah loh keh joh AH-gah)
📺 This phrase comes from the lyrics of a song by Alaska y Dinarama, later made popular by Thalía. It expresses a defiant

attitude toward social norms and other people's judgment.

Borró casette. - To erase the tape.
(boh-ROH kah-SEHT)
📺 From Maluma's song of the same title; used to fake amnesia.

TikTok Audios

Pintamos toda la casa. - We painted the whole house.
(peen-TAH-mohs TOH-dah lah KAH-sah)
📺 The whole audio is actually *"Pintamos toda la casa y sin dejar caer una sola gota de pintura que no sea... ¡¿Qué es ESO?!"*, and it's a TikTok audio that comes from the *SpongeBob SquarePants* show (*Bob Esponja* in Spanish). It is used when there is something or someone out of place in a situation.

Los peces son amigos, no comida. - Fish are friends, not food.
(lohs PEH-sehs sohn ah-MEE-gohs noh koh-MEE-dah)
📺 This phrase comes from *Finding Nemo* (*Buscando a Nemo* in Spanish) and it has become a viral TikTok audio to portray a situation when there is only one woman in a group of men.

Meme Culture

Se tenía que decir y se dijo. - It had to be said and it was said.
(seh teh-NYEE-ah keh deh-SEER ee seh DEE-hoh)
📺 This meme, which originated in a videogame, is used to express uncommon, unacceptable, or politically incorrect opinions.

No lo sé, Rick, parece falso. - I don't know, Rick, looks fake.
(noh loh SEH reek pah-REH-seh FAHL-soh)

📺 This meme was taken from the Spanish dubbing of Pawn Stars (*El precio de la historia* in Spanish) and is used when we believe someone is lying.

No sé qué sucederá pero estoy muy nervioso. - I don't know what will happen but I'm nervous.
(noh seh keh soo-seh-deh-RAH PEH-roh ehs-TOY mooy ne-hr-BYOH-soh)
📺 Another famous phrase and meme from *El precio de la historia.*

No, no, no... Bueno, sí. - No, no, no... well, yes.
(noh noh noh BWEH-noh see)
📺 This is one of **many** memes that come from the Spanish dubbing of *The Simpsons* (*Los Simpson* in Spanish). It is used to pretend that we don't want something or don't want to admit to something, but then end up admitting we do.

Qué agradable sujeto. - What a nice guy.
(keh ah-grah-DAH-bleh soo-HEH-toh)
📺 This is another meme from *Los Simpson*. Its meaning is usually straightforward to say that someone is a nice person, but it can also be used ironically at times.

Me quiero volver chango. - Sweet Merciful Crap.
(meh KYEH-roh bohl-BEHR CHAHN-goh)
📺 Another *Los Simpson* meme. This one is actually Homer's catchphrase "Sweet merciful crap" and is used regularly to curse when something goes wrong.

Es broma, pero si quieres no es broma - Just kidding, but if you want I'm not
(ehs BROH-mah, PEH-roh see KYEH-rehs noh ehs BROH-mah)
📺 This meme is used to say that the thing we said right before was meant as a joke, but if there is any possibility that

the other person wants to, then it isn't a joke. It is particularly used when flirting, but it can be used in any situation when we express something we want bluntly and jokingly.

Achis, achis, los mariachis. - Wow, wow, the mariachis.
(AH-chees AH-chees lohs mah-RYAH-chees)
📺 We use this expression when someone or something amazes us. 👁️➖👁️

Ájale, jalea. - Whoa, jelly.
(AH-hah-leh hah-LEH-ah)
📺 Funny Mexican phrase; said to react with amazement.

Oye, oye, más despacio, cerebrito. - Hey, hey, slow down, brainiac.
(OH-jeh OH-jeh mahs dehs-PAH-syoh seh-reh-BREE-toh)
📺 Yet another *Los Simpson* meme! This one is said by Chief Gorgory and is used when someone is explaining something too fast or in a manner that's too complicated, so we ask them to slow down.

Adoro los finales felices. - I love happy endings.
(ah-DOH-roh lohs fee-NAH-les feh-LEE-sehs)
📺 This meme comes from the Spanish dubbing of *The Fairly OddParents* (*Los padrinos mágicos* in Spanish) and is used literally when something actually has a happy ending.

Mi primera chamba. - My first job.
(mee pree-MEH-rah CHAHM-bah)
📺 This meme comes from an AI-generated song and video showing people having workplace bloopers. It now appears whenever an unexpected, funny, or epic situation happens on the job.

Tres doritos después... - Three Doritos later...
(trehs doh-REE-tohs dehs-PWEHS)

66

📺 This one comes from a Doritos commercial that showed bored people who ate three Doritos and then became active or started doing extreme things. Now, it's used to show or talk about a regular situation and then something unexpected that ends up happening.

¿Por qué me persigue la desgracia? - Why does misfortune chase me?
(pohr-KEH meh pehr-SEE-geh lah dehs-GRAH-syah)
📺 This *Los Simpsons* meme is used to be overly dramatic about something bad that happened to us, and is generally used as a joke.

Nada puede malir sal. - Nothing can possibly go wrong.
(NAH-dah PWEH-deh mah-LEER SAHL)
📺 This *Los Simpson* meme plays with the fact that someone is assuring someone else that nothing can go wrong, but does so by saying *salir* and *mal* wrongly. Now, it is used jokingly to encourage people that nothing can go wrong.

> **Between Cultures:** Keep in mind that the Spanish dubbing usually has two versions: the Latin American and the Spaniard one. This means you have to choose *Español latino* when you watch them!

Movies

¿Por la garrita? - Do you claw swear?
(pohr lah gah-RREE-tah)
📺 This phrase comes from the Spanish dubbing of *Brother Bear* (*Tierra de osos* in Spanish). In the film in Spanish, instead of making a "pinky" swear, they make a "claw" swear. And though us Latinos didn't even "pinky" swear before, now we do it *por la garrita.*

Houston, tenemos un problema. - Houston, we have a problem.
(HYOOS-tohn teh-NEH-mohs oon proh-BLEH-mah)
📺 This phrase, just like in English, was popularized by the film *Apollo 13*.

Mejor afuera que adentro. - Better out than in.
(meh-HOHR ah-FWEH-rah keh ah-DEHN-troh)
📺 This phrase comes from the Spanish dubbing of *Shrek*. The main character says this when he farts, and now it is basically used in the same way as Shrek.

Ohana significa familia. - Ohana means family.
(oh-HAH-nah seeg-nee-FEE-kah fah-MEE-lya)
📺 You probably recognize this one, it comes from *Lilo and Stitch* and it is widely used in Latin America when we want to say that we love our family, or we use it ironically to say that family sticks together no matter what.

Trabajando duro o durando en el trabajo. - Working hard or hardly working.

(trah-bah-HAHN-doh DOO-roh oh doo-RAHN-doh ehn ehl trah-BAH-hoh)

📺 This is another one from *Shrek* and it is used just like the phrase "working hard or hardly working" in English, and it literally means "working hard or lasting at work".

No ordenaste tu papeleo anoche. - You didn't file your paperwork last night.
(noh ohr-deh-NAHS-teh too pah-peh-LEH-oh ah-NOH-cheh)

📺 This iconic phrase is from *Monsters Inc.* and became viral even before "going viral" was a thing, partially because of the excellent delivery by the voice actress and partially because Roz's character is simply iconic.

Un gran poder conlleva una gran responsabilidad. - With great power comes great responsibility.
(oon grahn poh-DEHR kohn-JEH-Bah oo-nah grahn rehs-po-hn-sah-bee-lee-DAHD)

📺 This phrase is said to Peter Parker (a.K.a. Spider-Man) and we use it to be overly dramatic about our responsibilities.

Yo lo pensé, pero tú lo dijiste. - I thought it, but you said it.
(joh loh pehn-SEH PEH-roh too loh dee-HEES-teh)

📺 This is actually a conversation from *White Chicks* (¿Y dónde están las rubias? in Spanish) and it is particularly used when saying a hard truth while *chismeando*.

¿Ya merito llegamos? - Are we there yet?
(jah meh-REE-toh jeh-GAH-mohs)

📺 This is a *Shrek 2* phrase that Burro (Donkey) says incessantly when he wants to get to Muy Muy Lejano (Far Far Away). It is used in the same way during long trips.

Qué interesante, cuéntame más. - How interesting, tell me more.
(keh een-teh-reh-SAHN-teh KWEHN-tah-meh mahs)

This is a meme that came from the movie *Willy Wonka and the Chocolate Factory*. Actually, the phrase isn't said in the movie, but it was added to a still photo of Gene Wilder as Willy Wonka. This is used ironically when someone is saying something uninteresting.

Han pasado 84 años. - It's been 84 years.
(ahn pah-SAH-doh och-en-TAH kwah-TROH AH-nyohs)
📺 This phrase is from *Titanic*, and it's used to say that something took too long or that we've been waiting too long for something to happen.

💡 No Sabo Challenge

Want to use these memes and popular phrases? Watch one of the movies and *telenovelas* we've recommended and find one of the Spanish memes we taught you. Then, record yourself as you use the Spanish phrase! You can also use the TikTok audios and make a short video like the ones Spanish speakers usually make. Post your video on TikTok or Instagram with the hashtag #NoSaboChallenge!

Chapter 8:

Travel & Adventures

Getting There

¿Cómo llego al supermercado? - How do I get to the supermarket?
(KOH-moh JEH-goh ahl soo-pehr-mehr-KAH-doh)
🔍 Basic question for directions. Use it when you're lost or unsure.

¿Dónde está la casa de Santiago? - Where is Santiago's house?
(DOHN-deh ehs-TAH lah KAH-sah deh sahn-TYAH-goh)
🔍 Swap "Santiago" for any name!

¿Dónde queda el centro comercial? - Where is the shopping mall?
(DOHN-deh KEH-dah ehl SEHN-troh koh-mehr-SYAL)
🔍 You can use *queda* or **está** for locations.

¿Hay un banco por aquí? - Is there a bank around here?
(AH-y oon BAHN-koh pohr ah-KEE)
🔍 Super useful phrase—use ¿Hay...? to ask if there's something nearby.

¿Hay una farmacia cerca? - Is there a pharmacy nearby?
(AH-y OO-nah fahr-MAH-syah SEHR-kah)
🔍 A variation of the previous phrase.

¿El aeropuerto está lejos? -Is the airport far?
(ehl ah-eh-roh-PWEHR-toh ehs-TAH LEH-hohs)
🔍 Good to ask about distances.

¿Qué bus me lleva hasta la playa? - Which bus takes me to the beach?
(keh boos meh JEH-bah AHS-tah lah PLAH-jah)
🔄 You can also hear **camión**, **autobús** and **colectivo**, depending on the Spanish dialect.

Sigue derecho. - Go straight.
(SEE-geh deh-REH-choh)
🔍 Most common instruction you'll hear when asking for directions.

Gira a la izquierda. - Turn left.
(HEE-rah ah lah ees-KYEHR-dah)
🔍 You can also hear **dobla** instead of *gira*.

Dobla a la derecha. - Turn right.

(DOH-blah ah lah deh-REH-chah)
🔍 *La derecha* is also your right hand.

Camina tres cuadras. - Walk three blocks.
(kah-MEE-nah trehs KWAH-drahs)
🔍 *Cuadra* = block, standard measure for directions in Latin America.

Cruza la avenida. - Cross the avenue.
(KROO-sah lah ah-beh-NEE-dah)
🔍 Direct and simple—you'll hear this with **calle** (street) too.

Ve hasta la calle Entre Ríos. - Go to Entre Ríos Street.
(beh AHS-tah lah KAH-jeh EHN-treh REE-ohs)
🔍 Use it as a template and insert any street name.

Toma la primera salida. - Take the first exit.
(TOH-mah lah pree-MEH-rah sah-LEE-dah)
🔍 Especially useful on roundabouts or highways.

Está a la vuelta de la esquina. - It's around the corner.
(ehs-TAH ah lah BWEHL-tah deh lah ehs-KEE-nah)
🔍 Don't take it literally; it's used to indicate that something is close by.

Está en la calle Laja entre Osorio y Lima. - It's on Laja Street, between Osorio and Lima.
(ehs-TAH ehn lah KAH-jeh LAH-hah EHN-treh oh-SOH-ryoh ee LEE-mah)
🔍 The way to describe an address with cross streets.

Disculpa, no soy de aquí. - Sorry, I'm not from here.
(dees-KOOL-pah noh soy deh ah-KEE)
🔍 Polite way to admit you can't help with directions.

Between Cultures: In the US, many towns and suburbs are built for cars first: wide highways, big parking lots, and long distances between shops or schools. Walking isn't always practical, and public transportation can be limited. However, in Latin America, many cities are much more walkable. Streets are narrower, markets and stores are close together, and it's common to see people doing daily errands on foot. Public transportation (like buses, subways, or buses) also plays a big role.

At the Airport

¿Tiene su pasaporte? - Do you have your passport?
(TYEH-neh soo pah-sah-POHR-teh)
🔍 Always the first question at check-in or border control.

¿A qué hora es el vuelo? - What time is the flight?
(ah keh OH-rah ehs ehl BWEH-loh)
🔍 A must-ask when confirming travel plans.

¿Con qué aerolínea vuela? - Which airline are you flying with?
(kohn keh ah-eh-roh-LEE-nyah BWEH-lah)
🔍 Useful when staff need to direct you to the right counter.

¿Viaja por negocios o por placer? - Are you traveling for business or pleasure?
(BYAH-hah pohr neh-GOH-syohs oh por plah-SEHR)
🔍 A standard customs or immigration question.

¿Dónde se hospedará? - Where will you be staying?
(DOHN-deh seh ohs-peh-dah-RAH)
🔍 Another standard question asked at immigration for entry records.

¿Cuánto dinero en efectivo trae consigo? - How much cash are you carrying with you?
(KWAHN-toh dee-NEH-roh ehn eh-fehk-TEE-boh TRAH-eh kohn-SEE-goh)
🔍 Remember, you can't travel with more than 10,000 USD in cash.

¿Tiene algo que declarar en aduanas? - Do you have anything to declare at customs?
(TYEH-neh AHL-goh keh deh-klah-RAHR ehn ah-DWAH-nahs)
🔍 Key question when crossing international borders.

Su puerta de embarque es la número 10. - Your boarding gate is number 10.
(soo PWEHR-tah deh ehm-BAHR-keh ehs lah NOO-meh-roh DYEHS)
🔍 You don't want to miss your flight!

Debe hacer el control de seguridad. - You must go through the security check.
(DEH-beh ah-SEHR el kohn-TROHL deh seh-goo-ree-DAHD)
🔍 Standard airport procedure for all passengers

Su boleto solo incluye equipaje de mano. - Your ticket only includes carry-on luggage.
(soo boh-LEH-toh SOH-loh een-KLOO-jeh eh-kee-PAH-heh deh MAH-noh)
🔄 They might alternatively use the words **pasaje** or **ticket**.

¿Debo despachar mi maleta? - Should I check my suitcase?
(DEH-boh dehs-pah-CHAR mee mah-LEH-tah)
🔄 Some countries use the word **valija**.

Este es el último llamado del vuelo 235... - This is the last call for flight 235...
(EHS-teh ehs ehl OOL-tee-moh jah-MAH-doh dehl BWEH-loh dohs trehs SEEN-koh)
🔍 If 235 is your flight, you better star running!

¿Cuál es mi asiento? - Which one is my seat?
(kwahl ehs mee ah-SYEHN-toh)
🔍 You can ask the flight attendant if you are in doubt.

¿Prefiere asiento de ventanilla o pasillo? - Do you prefer a window or aisle seat?
(preh-FYEH-reh ah-SYEHN-toh deh behn-tah-NEE-jah oh pah-SEE-joh)
🔍 The eternal flight dilemma.

Abróchense el cinturón de seguridad. -Fasten your seatbelt.
(ah-BROH-chehn-seh ehl seen-too-ROHN deh seh-goo-ree-DAHD)
🔍 You better know this safety instruction.

Pongan sus celulares en modo avión. - Put your cellphones on airplane mode.
(POHN-gahn soos seh-loo-LAH-rehs ehn MOH-doh ah-BYOHN)
🔍 You don't want to cause any interference!

Permanezcan sentados. - Remain seated.
(pehr-mah-NEHS-kahn sehn-TAH-dohs)
🔍 During takeoff, turbulence and landing.

No está permitido fumar. - Smoking is not allowed.
(noh ehs-TAH pehr-mee-TEE-doh foo-MAHR)
🔍 Standard rule on all commercial flights.

Mantengan el respaldo de su asiento en posición vertical. -
Keep your seatback in the upright position.
(mahn-TEHN-gahn ehl rehs-PAHL-doh deh soo ah-SYEHN-
toh ehn poh-see-SYOHN behr-tee-KAHL)
🔍 Another safety announcement during takeoff and landing.

En este avión hay 8 salidas de emergencia. - This plane has
8 emergency exits.
(ehn EHS-teh ah-BYOHN AH-y OH-choh sah-LEE-dahs deh
eh-mehr-HEN-syah)
🔍 Check which one is closest to you!

Colóquense su máscara de oxígeno. - Put on your oxygen
mask.
(koh-LOH-kehn-seh soo MAHS-kah-rah deh ohk-SEE-heh-
noh)
🔍 Do it before helping others.

¿Hay Wi-Fi disponible? - Is there Wi-Fi available?
(AH-y WAHY-fahy dees-poh-NEE-bleh)
🔍 Many flights now offer it.

Gracias por volar con nosotros. - Thank you for flying with
us.
(GRAH-syahs pohr boh-LAHR kohn noh-SOH-trohs)
🔍 The polite closing message of every airline.

Hay un poco de turbulencia. - There is a bit of turbulence.

(AH-y oon POH-koh deh toor-boo-LEHN-syah)
🔍 Nothing to worry about.

¿Dónde puedo alquilar un coche? - Where can I rent a car?
(DOHN-deh PWEH-doh ahl-kee-LAHR oon KOH-cheh)
🔍 Common question at the arrivals hall.

¿Dónde puedo recoger mi equipaje? - Where can I pick up my luggage?
(DOHN-deh PWEH-doh reh-koh-HEHR mee eh-kee-PAH-heh)
🔍 Standard at baggage claim after a flight.

He perdido mi equipaje. - I have lost my luggage.
(eh pehr-DEE-doh mee eh-kee-PAH-heh)
🔍 We hope you don't need to say this!

JOIN OUR FREE SPANISH COMMUNITY
TO SOUND MORE NATURAL, LEARN FROM EXPERTS, AND LISTEN TO ALL THE PHRASES NARRATED VIA AN AUDIBLE FREE TRIAL!

SCAN THE QR CODE
— OR —
visit **bit.ly/4sUdr6f**

Tourism

Hay un tour guiado a las 15. - There is a guided tour at 3 p.m.
(AH-y oon toor gee-AH-doh ah lahs KEEN-seh)
🔍 Latinos use both the 12-hour (a.m./p.m.) and the 24-hour methods for time.. The latter is what you would refer to as "military time" in the US.

La entrada al museo es gratuita. - Admission to the museum is free of charge.
(lah ehn-TRAH-dah ahl moo-SEH-oh ehs grah-TWEE-tah)
🔍 Museums sometimes offer free admission on specific days.

El guía nos mostrará los mejores lugares. - The guide will show us the best places.
(ehl GEE-ah nohs mohs-trah-RAH lohs meh-HOH-rehs loo-GAH-rehs)
🔍 Guides know local secrets you might miss on your own.

Visitemos el casco histórico. - Let's visit the historic center.
(bee-see-TEH-mohs ehl KAHS-koh ees-TOH-ree-koh)
🔍 *Casco histórico* usually refers to the old part of town.

Me gustaría visitar la catedral. - I would like to visit the cathedral.
(meh goos-tah-REE-ah bee-see-TAHR lah kah-teh-DRAHL)
🔍 Cathedrals are often at the *casco histórico*.

Saqué un boleto de ida y vuelta. - I got a round-trip ticket.
(sah-KEH oon boh-LEH-toh deh EE-dah ee BWEHL-tah)
🔍 When you are not planning on staying forever!

Hay un mercado muy bonito por aquí. - There is a very nice market around here.
(AH-y oon mehr-KAH-doh mooy boh-NEE-toh por ah-KEE)
🔍 Markets are the best place to taste local food.

Es un gran día para ir a la playa. - It's a great day to go to the beach.
(ehs oon grahn DEE-ah PAH-rah eer ah lah PLAH-jah)
🔍 Every day is a great day to go to the beach!

Tomaremos un ferry hasta la isla. - We will take a ferry to the island.
(toh-mah-REH-mohs oon FEH-rree ahs-tah lah EES-lah)
🔍 *Ferry* comes from the English word, just roll your R to sound more natural in Spanish.

El bus nos buscará para la excursión a las 10. - The bus will pick us up for the tour at 10.
(ehl boos nohs boos-kah-RAH PAH-rah lah eks-koor-SYON ah lahs dyehs)
🔍 *Excursión* usually means a day trip, often organized.

¡Mira! Hay unas tortugas marinas allí. - Look! There are some sea turtles over there.
(MEE-rah AH-y OO-nahs tohr-TOO-gahs mah-REE-nahs ah-JEE)
🔍 Spotting animals in the wild is always a highlight of any trip.

At the Hotel

Tengo una reserva a nombre de López. - I have a reservation under the name López.
(TEHN-goh OO-nah reh-SEHR-bah ah NOHM-breh deh LOH-pehs)
🔍 Hotels will always ask for the name on the booking.

¿Quiere una habitación simple o doble? - Do you want a single or double room?
(KYEH-reh OO-nah ah-bee-tah-SYON SEEM-pleh oh DOH-bleh)
🔍 *Simple* = single, *doble* = double. Easy to remember.

¿A qué hora es el check-in? - What time is check-in?
(ah keh OH-rah ehs ehl chehk-EEN)
🔍 *Check-in* is borrowed from English!

¿Está incluido el desayuno? - Is breakfast included?
(ehs-TAH een-kloo-EE-doh ehl deh-sah-JOO-noh)
🔍 Hopefully it's a *desayuno continental*!

Quisiera una habitación con vista al mar. - I would like a room with an ocean view.
(kee-SYEH-rah OO-nah ah-bee-tah-SYON kohn BEES-tah ahl MAHR)
🔍 A classic request at beach destinations.

¿Pueden darme una habitación silenciosa? - Can you give me a quiet room?
(PWEH-den DAHR-meh OO-nah ah-bee-tah-SYOHN see-lehn-SYOH-sah)
🔍 Great phrase if you're a light sleeper.

¿Hay habitaciones disponibles para esta noche? - Are there rooms available for tonight?
(AH-y ah-bee-tah-SYOH-nes dees-poh-NEE-blehs PAH-rah EHS-tah NOH-cheh)
🔍 Useful if you didn't book in advance.

Necesito una habitación para dos personas. - I need a room for two.
(neh-seh-SEE-toh OO-nah ah-bee-tah-SYON PAH-rah dohs pehr-SOH-nahs)
🔍 Or you can ask for **una habitación doble**.

¿Cuál es la contraseña del Wi-Fi? - What is the Wi-Fi password?
(kwahl ehs lah kohn-trah-SEH-nyah dehl WAHY-fahy)

✏️ "Wi-Fi" is also pronounced "WEE-fee" in Spanish.

¿Dónde está el spa? - Where is the spa?
(DOHN-deh ehs-TAH ehl spah)
🔍 Most hotels have a spa or wellness center.

¿Hay servicio de lavandería? - Is there laundry service?
(AH-y sehr-BEE-syoh deh lah-bahn-deh-REE-ah)
🔍 Perfect if you're traveling light.

¿Se puede pedir comida a la habitación? - Can I order room service?
(seh PWEH-deh peh-DEER koh-MEE-dah ah lah ah-bee-tah-SYON)
🔍 Larger hotels tend to have room service.

¿El hotel ofrece transporte al aeropuerto? - Does the hotel offer airport transfer?
(ehl oh-TEHL oh-FREH-seh trahns-POHR-teh ahl ah-eh-roh-PWEHR-toh)
🔍 If it doesn't, you can take a **taxi**, spelled and pronounced just like in English!

¿Dónde puedo estacionar mi coche? - Where can I park my car?
(DOHN-deh PWEH-doh ehs-tah-syoh-NAR mee KOH-cheh)
🔍 *Coche* means car; in Latin America, you might also hear **carro** or **auto**.

¿Puedo dejar mi equipaje antes del check-in? - Can I leave my luggage before check-in?
(PWEH-doh deh-HAR mee eh-kee-PAH-heh AHN-tehs dehl chehk-EEN)
🔍 Leave your luggage and start enjoying the city!

Necesito toallas adicionales. - I need extra towels.

(neh-seh-SEE-toh toh-AH-jahs ah-dee-syoh-NAH-lehs)
🔍 Learn the verb *necesito* (to need) and use it to ask for things.

La habitación no está limpia. - The room is not clean.
(lah ah-bee-tah-SYON noh ehs-TAH LEEM-pyah)
🔍 Polite but direct way to ask for housekeeping.

No funciona el aire acondicionado. - The air conditioning doesn't work.
(noh foon-SYOH-nah ehl AHI-reh ah-kohn-dee-syoh-NAH-doh)
🔍 Essential phrase in hot climates.

El baño tiene un problema con el agua caliente. - The bathroom has a problem with the hot water.
(ehl BAH-nyoh TYEH-neh oon proh-BLEH-mah kohn ehl AH-gwah kah-LYEN-teh)
🔍 A common issue in older hotels.

La llave no abre la puerta. - The key doesn't open the door.
(lah JAH-beh noh AH-breh lah PWEHR-tah)
🔍 If it's a card, they might need to reprogram it.

Perdí la tarjeta de la habitación. - I lost the room key card.
(pehr-DEE lah tahr-HEH-tah deh lah ah-bee-tah-SYON)
🔍 They'll usually give you a new one right away.

Hay demasiado ruido en el pasillo. - There is too much noise in the hallway.
(AH-y deh-mah-SYAH-doh RWEE-doh ehn ehl pah-SEE-joh)
🔍 Don't hesitate to complain.

Quisiera cambiar de habitación. - I would like to change rooms.
(kee-SYEH-rah kahm-BYAR deh ah-bee-tah-SYON)
🔍 Hotels are used to this kind of request.

Quisiera hacer el check-out. - I would like to check out.
(kee-SYEH-rah ah-SEHR ehl chek-OUT)
🔍 Check-out is usually at noon.

¿Puedo dejar mi equipaje hasta la tarde? - Can I leave my luggage until the afternoon?
(PWEH-doh deh-HAR mee eh-kee-PAH-heh AHS-tah lah TA-HR-deh)
🔍 Do you have an afternoon flight? This phrase will come in handy.

Gracias por su atención. - Thank you for your attention.
(GRAH-syahs pohr soo ah-tehn-SYOHN)
🔍 This is a polite phrase to end any request.

Espero que hayan disfrutado su estadía. - I hope you enjoyed your stay.
(ehs-PEH-roh keh AH-yahn dees-froo-TAH-doh soo ehs-tah-DEE-ah)
🔍 You will hear this from hotel staff at check-out.

Lamentamos las molestias. - We apologize for the inconvenience.
(lah-men-TAH-mohs lahs moh-LES-tyahs)
🔍 Standard hotel and restaurant response when something goes wrong.

Camping

¿Sueles ir de campamento? - Do you usually go camping?
(SWEH-lehs eer deh kahm-pah-MEHN-toh)
🔍 Great opener for outdoorsy conversations.

¿Sabes hacer fuego? - Do you know how to
make a fire?
(SAH-behs ah-SEHR FWEH-goh)
🔍 It's a useful skill for camping trips.

Ve a buscar leña y yesca para el fuego. - Go get firewood
and tinder for the fire.
(beh ah boos-KAHR LEH-nyah ee JEHS-kah PAH-rah ehl
FWEH-goh)
🔍 You can also make a ***fogata*** (bonfire).

Llena la cantimplora en el arroyo. - Fill the canteen in the
stream.
(JEH-nah lah kahn-teem-PLOH-rah ehn ehl ah-ROH-joh)
🔍 Don't forget to hydrate while outdoors.

Hierve el agua antes de tomarla. - Boil the water before
drinking it.
(YEHR-beh ehl AH-gwah AHN-tehs deh toh-MAHR-lah)
🔍 You don't want to get sick!

Este es un buen lugar para armar la tienda. - This is a good
place to set up the tent.
(EHS-teh ehs oon bwehn loo-GAR PAH-rah ahr-MAHR lah
TYEHN-dah)
🔍 Choosing the spot is key.

Clava la estaca con una piedra. - Drive the stake with a
rock.

(CLAH-bah lah ehs-TAH-kah kon OO-nah PYEH-drah)
🔍 Practical camping instruction.

¿Quieres ir a pescar al río? - Do you want to go fishing at the river?
(KYEH-res eer ah pehs-CAR al REE-oh)
🔍 Fishing is a fun camping activity.

Mi mochila es de 45 litros. - My backpack is 45 liters.
(mee moh-CHEE-lah ehs deh kwah-REHN-tah ee SEEN-koh LEE-trohs)
🔍 Backpacks are measured in liquid capacity.

¿Tienes un encendedor? - Do you have a lighter?
(TYEH-nehs oon ehn-sehn-deh-DOHR)
🔍 Always useful outdoors, but remember to put out the fire afterwards.

Apunta aquí con la linterna. - Point the flashlight here.
(ah-POON-tah ah-KEE kon lah leen-TEHR-nah)
🔍 Handy phrase at night.

Cierra el mosquitero que hay insectos. - Close the mosquito net, there are bugs.
(SYEH-rrah ehl mohs-kee-TEH-roh keh AH-y een-SEHK-tos)
🔍 *Mosquitos* and *moscas* (flies) are the most typical insects during camping.

Este sendero no es para principiantes. - This trail is not for beginners.
(EHS-teh sehn-DEH-roh noh ehs PAH-rah preen-see-PYAHN-tehs)
🔍 If you are in a Spanish-speaking country, pay attention to signs. Green usually means that the trail is easy.

Necesitas equipo de escalada. - You need climbing gear.

(neh-seh-SEE-tahs eh-KEE-poh deh ehs-kah-LAH-dah)
🔍 For more advanced adventures.

¿Me prestas tu navaja suiza? - Can I borrow your Swiss knife?
(meh PREHS-tahs too nah-BAH-hah SWEE-sah)
🔍 *Navaja suiza* = swiss knife; **cortaplumas** = penknife.

¿Sabes hacia dónde vamos? - Do you know where we're going?
(SAH-behs AH-syah DOHN-deh BAH-mohs)
🔍 Useful when hiking with friends.

Ya pasamos por aquí antes. - We've been through here before.
(jah pah-SAH-mohs pohr ah-KEE AHN-tehs)
🔍 A common sign you're lost.

Estamos yendo en círculos. - We're going in circles.
(ehs-TAH-mos YEN-doh en SEER-koo-lohs)
🔍 If you are walking in circles, better ask for help..

Creo que nos perdimos... - I think we are lost...
(KREH-oh keh nohs pehr-DEE-mohs)
🔍 Every explorer has said this at least once.

💡 No Sabo Challenge

Are you travelling to a Spanish-speaking country or are you going camping? Record some interactions with locals and try to use the phrases we've taught you. If you're going camping, record yourself as you set up camp and use some key phrases. Then, post your video on TikTok or Instagram (with the person's permission, of course) with the hashtag #NoSaboChallenge!

Chapter 9

Jobs and Professions

General Phrases

Soy un/una nómade digital. - I'm a digital nomad.
(soy oon/OO-nah NOH-mah-deh dee-hee-TAHL)
Living life with Wi-Fi and sunshine!

Trabajo desde mi casa. - I work from home.
(trah-BAH-hoh DEHS-deh mee KAH-sah)
Pajamas are the new office attire.

Soy diseñador/diseñadora web. - I am a web designer.
(soy dee-seh-nyah-DOHR/dee-seh-nyah-DOH-rah web)
Pixels and creativity all day long!

Voy a la universidad. - I go to college.
(boy ah lah oo-nee-behr-see-DAHD)
Brain upgrade in progress.

Tengo una reunión en 5 minutos. - I have a meeting in 5 minutes.
(TEN-goh OO-nah rew-NYOHN ehn SEEN-koh mee-NOO-tohs)
Quick, grab your coffee!

Mi padre es fontanero. - My father is a plumber.
(mee PAH-dreh ehs fon-tah-NEH-roh)
You can also say **plomero**.

Between Cultures: Did you know there are many words we can use to talk about your *trabajo*? In Argentina and Uruguay, it's ***laburo,*** from the Italian word *lavorare*. In Mexico, Ecuador, and Central American countries, it's ***chamba***. The related verbs are ***laburar***, ***chambear***. In Mexico, someone who is very ***jalador*** or ***jaladora*** is a person who enthusiastically joins a common endeavor. We also have the word ***jale*** as work and ***jalar*** as equivalent to *trabajar*.

Usual Questions

¿De qué trabaja tu madre? - What does your mother do for work?
(deh keh trah-BAH-hah too MAH-dreh)
💼 Always curious, never nosy.

¿Tu hermano es economista? - Is your brother an economist?
(too ehr-MAH-noh ehs eh-koh-noh-MEES-tah)
💼 Numbers, charts, and endless spreadsheets.

¿Qué haces en tu trabajo? - What do you do at your job?
(keh AH-sehs ehn too trah-BAH-hoh)
💼 The classic small-talk starter.

¿Dónde queda tu oficina? - Where is your office located?
(DOHN-deh KEH-dah too oh-fee-SEE-nah)
💼 Hopefully near good coffee shops.

¿Cuál es tu horario de trabajo? - What is your work schedule?
(KWAHL ehs too oh-RAH-ryoh deh trah-BAH-hoh)
💼 Nine-to-five... or twenty-four-seven?

¿Qué harás durante el almuerzo? - What will you do during lunch?

(keh ah-RAHS doo-RAHN-teh ehl al-MWEHR-soh)
💼Tacos? Salad? Nap? Choices, choices.

¿Con qué tarea estás hoy? - What task are you working on today?
(kohn keh tah-REH-ah ehs-TAHS oy)
💼One task at a time... maybe.

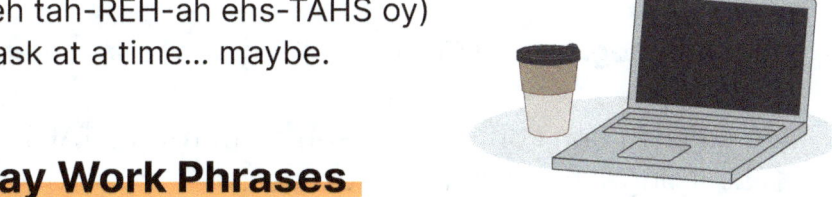

Everyday Work Phrases

Tengo una entrega mañana por la mañana. - I have a deadline tomorrow morning.
(TEN-goh OO-nah en-TREH-gah mah-NYAH-nah pohr lah mah-NYAH-nah)
💼 Coffee will be your best friend.

Estoy muy atrasado/atrasada. - I am very behind.
(ehs-TOY mooy ah-trah-SAH-doh)
💼 Don't worry, you've got this!

Hoy tendré que hacer horas extra. - Today I'll have to work overtime.
(oy ten-DREH keh ah-SEHR OH-rahs EHKS-trah)
💼 More hours, more coffee.

No llegaré a la entrega de la semana que viene. - I won't make the deadline next week.
(noh jeh-gah-REH ah lah en-TREH-gah deh lah seh-MAH-nah keh BYEH-neh)
💼 Deadlines love to play hide and seek.

Tengo una entrevista de trabajo. - I have a job interview.
(TEN-goh OO-nah en-treh-BEES-tah deh trah-BAH-hoh)
💼 Time to shine like a superstar!

Mañana tenemos una conferencia. - Tomorrow we have a conference.

(mah-NYAH-nah teh-NEH-mohs OO-nah kohn-feh-REHN-syah)

💼 Bring your notes and your best smile.

Iré a un congreso en Bogotá. - I'm going to a conference in Bogotá.

(ee-REH ah oon kohn-GREH-soh en boh-goh-TAH)

💼 Learning + networking = success.

Estoy con mucho trabajo. - I have a lot of work.

(ehs-TOY kohn MOO-choh trah-BAH-hoh)

💼 Work hard, rest harder.

💡 No Sabo Challenge

Do you work with some bilingual Americans or Latin American immigrants? Use some of the phrases you've learned during your lunch break or at work and see what happens! Then, post your video on TikTok or Instagram (with the person's permission, of course) with the hashtag #NoSaboChallenge. Look up the hashtag to see how other workers have done.

Chapter 10

Typical *Abuela* Sayings

Al que madruga, Dios lo ayuda. - The early bird gets the worm.
(ahl keh mah-DROO-gah dyohs loh ah-JOO-dah)
👵 Literally, "God helps those who rise early"; grandmas say this to push you out of bed.

Más sabe el diablo por viejo que por diablo. - Wisdom comes with age.
(Mahs SAH-beh el DYAH-bloh por BYEH-ho keh por DYAH-bloh)
👵 Literally, "The devil knows more because he's old than because he's the devil". Experience always beats cunning.

Un día me vas a matar de un susto. - One day you'll give me a heart attack.
(oon DEE-ah meh bahs ah mah-TAHR deh oon SOOS-toh)
👵 A dramatic way to scold you.

Guarda esas lágrimas para cuando me muera. - Save those tears for when I'm gone.
(GWAHR-dah EH-sahs LAH-gree-mahs PAH-rah KWAHN-doh meh MWEH-rah)
👵 A classic guilt-trip phrase.

Me tenías con el Jesús en la boca. - You had me so worried!
(meh teh-NEE-ahs kohn ehl heh-SOOS ehn lah BOH-kah)
👵 A religious twist on "You scared me to death;" literally:

"You had me with Jesus in my mouth."

Me vas a sacar canas verdes. - You're going to drive me crazy.
(meh BAHS ah sah-KAHR KAH-nahs BEHR-dehs)
👵 A colorful way to say "You're stressing me out."

A buen entendedor, pocas palabras. - A word to the wise is enough.
(ah bwehn ehn-tehn-deh-DOHR POH-kahs pah-LAH-brahs)
👵 Grandma's way of saying "Don't make me repeat myself."

A caballo regalado no se le miran los dientes. - Don't look a gift horse in the mouth.
(ah kah-BAH-joh reh-gah-LAH-doh noh seh leh MEE-rahn lohs DYEN-tehs)
👵 Be grateful for what you get.

No hay mal que por bien no venga. - Every cloud has a silver lining.
(noh AH-y mahl keh pohr byehn noh BEHN-gah)
👵 Optimism, *abuela*-style.

Camarón que se duerme, se lo lleva la corriente. - You snooze, you lose.
(kah-mah-ROHN keh seh DWER-meh, seh loh YEH-bah lah koh-RRYEHN-teh)
🔄 Literally, "A shrimp that falls asleep is carried away by the current". There's a variant that goes **Cocodrilo que duerme, es cartera** ("A crocodile that falls asleep is turned into a purse").

Cría cuervos y te sacarán los ojos. - Raise ravens and they'll peck your eyes out.
(KREE-ah KWEHR-bohs ee teh sah-kah-RAHN lohs OH-hos)
👵 It's similar to English saying "Lie down with dogs, wake up with fleas," but much darker!

Dios los cría y el viento los amontona. - Birds of a feather flock together.
(DYOS lohs KREE-ah ee el BYEHN-toh lohs ah-mohn-TOH-nah)

👵 As is common in Spanish, God appears in this *abuela* saying.

Más vale prevenir que curar. - Better safe than sorry.
(mahs BAH-leh preh-beh-NEER keh koo-RAHR)

👵 Classic advice before you leave the house without a sweater.

A palabras necias, oídos sordos. - Ignore foolish words.
(ah pah-LAH-brahs NEH-syahs, oh-EE-dohs SOHR-dohs)

👵 Don't waste time on nonsense.

En boca cerrada no entran moscas. - Silence is golden.
(ehn BOH-kah seh-RRAH-dah noh EHN-trahn MOHS-kahs)

👵 Better not to talk too much; literally, "Flies don't enter a closed mouth."

El que busca, encuentra. - Seek and you shall find.
(ehl keh BOOS-kah, ehn-KWEHN-trah)
🧓 Grandma's way of saying "Don't give up."

Ladran, Sancho (señal que cabalgamos). - Let the dogs bark, Sancho. It is a sign that we're moving forward.
(LAH-drahn, SAHN-choh seh-NYAHL keh kah-bahl-GAH-mohs)
🧓 Quoting Don Quixote to keep going despite criticism.

Between Cultures: Some sayings come from important books in Latin American history like *La Biblia*, *Don Quijote* or *Martín Fierro*. You can try to read a bilingual edition to practice your Spanish!

De tal palo tal astilla. - Like father, like son.
(deh tahl PAH-loh tahl ahs-TEE-jah)
🧓Used when you act just like your parents.

En casa de herrero, cuchillo de palo. - The shoemaker's son goes barefoot.
(ehn KAH-sah deh eh-RREH-roh, koo-CHEE-joh deh PAH-loh)
🧓Experts often neglect themselves.

No hay peor ciego que el que no quiere ver. - There's none so blind as those who won't see.
(noh AH-y peh-OHR SYEH-goh keh ehl keh noh KYEH-reh BEHR)
🧓A truth bomb about denial.

El que no corre, vuela. - First come, first served.
(ehl keh noh KOH-rreh, BWEH-lah)
🧓It ironically refers to those who get ahead of others to obtain benefits or take opportunities.

Hazte la fama y échate a dormir. - Get a reputation and

then relax.
(AHS-teh lah FAH-mah ee EH-chah-teh ah dohr-MEER)
🧓Once people know you for something, it sticks.

Del dicho al hecho hay mucho trecho. - Easier said than done.
(dehl DEE-choh ahl EH-choh AH-y MOO-choh TREH-choh)
🧓Grandma's way of saying "Talk is cheap."

El que calla otorga. - Silence is consent.
(ehl keh KAH-jah oh-TOHR-gah)
🧓 If you don't speak up, people assume you agree.

Donde hubo fuego, cenizas quedan. - Where once there was fire, ashes remain.
(DOHN-deh OO-boh FWEH-goh, seh-NEE-sahs KEH-dahn)
🧓 It's used to say that after a strong emotion, such as love or anger, there are always something left behind.

Dime con quién andas y te diré quién eres. - Tell me who your friends are and I'll tell you who you are.
(DEE-meh kohn KYEHN AHN-dahs ee teh dee-REH KYEHN EH-rehs)
🧓 Who you spend time with says a lot about you.

El que ríe último ríe mejor. - He who laughs last, laughs best.
(ehl keh REE-eh OOL-tee-moh REE-eh meh-HOR)
🧓 Patience pays off, similar to English "Revenge is a dish best served cold."

El que no llora, no mama. - The squeaky wheel gets the grease.
(ehl keh noh JOH-rah, noh MAH-mah)
🧓 If you don't ask for it, you don't get it.

Aunque la mona se vista de seda, mona se queda. - You

can't make a silk puse out of a sow's ear.
(AH-oon-keh lah MOH-nah seh BEES-tah deh SEH-dah MOH-nah seh KEH-dah)
 Fancy clothes don't change who you are. Literally, "If a monkey dresses in silk, it's still a monkey."

Más vale pájaro en mano que cien volando. - A bird in the hand is worth two in the bush.
(mahs BAH-leh PAH-hah-roh ehn MAH-noh keh SYEN boh-LAN-doh)
 Better hold onto what you have.

Ojos que no ven, corazón que no siente. - Out of sight, out of mind.
(OH-hos keh noh BEN koh-rah-SOHN keh noh SYEN-teh)
 It has two meaning: distance makes it easier to forget, and what you don't know can't hurt you.

💡 No Sabo Challenge

Ask your *abuela* (or any older family member) to tell you their favorite Spanish sayings or *dichos* and try to guess the English equivalent. Record the whole interaction and post your video on TikTok or Instagram with the hashtag #NoSaboChallenge. Check how other families are sharing their *abuela* sayings!

Chapter 11:

People

Body

Mi hermano es alto. - My brother is tall.
(mee ehr-MAH-noh ehs AHL-toh)
👨‍👩 He can probably reach the top shelf without a chair.

Sofía es bajita. - Sofía is short.
(soh-FEE-ah ehs bah-HEE-tah)
✏️ The adjective is *bajo/baja*, but the *-ito/-ita* ending is a diminutive (it adds a nuance of being small).

Tengo los ojos verdes. - I have green eyes.
(TEHN-goh lohs OH-hohs BEHR-dehs)
👨‍👩 Like small emeralds.

Luis está muy delgado, ¿no? - Luis is very thin, isn't he?
(lwees ehs-TAH mooy del-GAH-doh, noh)
👨‍👩 Slim like a supermodel.

La actriz es hermosa. - The actress is beautiful.
(lah ahk-TREES ehs ehr-MOH-sah)
👨‍👩 Hollywood vibes all the way.

Eres muy buenmozo. - You are very handsome.
(EH-rehs mooy bwehn-MOH-soh)
✏️ *Buenmozo* is used for men, not women.

99

¡Qué feo eres! - How ugly you are!
(keh FEH-oh EH-rehs)
👨‍👩‍👧 Ouch... hopefully said as a joke.

Es un hombre gordo. - He is a fat man.
(ehs oon OHM-breh GOHR-doh)
👨‍👩‍👧 Big body, big personality.

Hay muchas personas obesas en mi ciudad. - There are many obese people in my city.
(AH-y MOO-chahs pehr-SOH-nahs oh-BEH-sahs en mee syoo-DAHD)
👨‍👩‍👧 A social observation, no judgment.

El hombre es musculoso. - The man is muscular.
(ehl OHM-breh ehs moos-koo-LOH-soh)
👨‍👩‍👧 Looks like he lives at the gym.

Mi tía es rellenita. - My aunt is chubby.
(mee TEE-ah ehs rreh-jeh-NEE-tah)
👨‍👩‍👧 Extra hugs guaranteed.

Carlos tiene la piel clara. - Carlos has fair skin.
(KAHR-lohs TYEH-neh lah pyehl KLAH-rah)
👨‍👩‍👧 Pale and proud.

Mariana tiene la piel morena. - Mariana has dark skin.
(mah-RYAH-nah TYEH-neh lah pyehl moh-REH-nah)
👨‍👩‍👧 Black and proud!

Between Cultures: Just like North America, Central and South America are two very diverse continents regarding ethnicity due to colonization, slavery, and migratory waves at different points in history. So if someone tells you there aren't any white Latinos, tell them they're wrong!

Hairstyles

Roberto tiene el cabello corto. - Roberto has short hair.
(ro-BEHR-toh TYEH-neh ehl kah-BEH-joh KOHR-toh)
👨‍👧 Low maintenance, high style.

Julia tiene el cabello largo. - Julia has long hair.
(HOO-lyah TYEH-neh ehl kah-BEH-joh LAHR-goh)
👨‍👧 Rapunzel, is that you?

La niña lleva coleta. - The girl wears a ponytail.
(lah NEE-nyah YEH-bah koh-LEH-tah)
👨‍👧 Classic and cute hairstyle.

¿Tomás es rubio? - Is Tomás blond?
(toh-MAHS ehs RROO-byoh)
👨‍👧 Blonde squad check.

Mi hermana es castaña. - My sister has brown hair.
(mee ehr-MAH-nah ehs kahs-TAH-nyah)
👨‍👧 A lovely color.

La joven tiene rastas. - The young woman has dreadlocks.
(lah HOH-behn TYEH-neh RRAHS-tahs)
👨‍👧 Cool and alternative vibe.

Valeria tiene el cabello rizado. - Valeria has curly hair.
(bah-LEH-ryah TYEH-neh ehl kah-BEH-joh rree-SAH-doh)
🔄 You can also say **crespo** or **con rulos**.

Mateo tiene el pelo lacio. - Mateo has straight hair.
(mah-TEH-oh TYEH-neh ehl PEH-loh LAH-syoh)
👨‍👧 Sleek and smooth.

¡Papá ya tiene canas! - Dad already has gray hairs!
(pah-PAH yah TYEH-neh KAH-nahs)

👩‍👩‍👧 Wisdom highlights.

¿Te gusta mi cresta? - Do you like my mohawk?
(teh GOOS-tah mee KREHS-tah)
👩‍👩‍👧 Punk vibes activated.

Mi hijo tiene el cabello rapado. - My son has a shaved head.
(mee EE-hoh TYEH-neh ehl kah-BEH-yoh rah-PAH-doh)
👩‍👩‍👧 Practical and fresh.

El abuelo es calvo. - Grandpa is bald.
(ehl ah-BWEH-loh ehs KAHL-boh)
🔄 In South America, it's ***pelado***.

Clara se pintó el cabello de rojo. - Clara dyed her hair red.
(KLAH-rah seh peen-TOH ehl kah-BEH-joh deh ROH-hoh)
👩‍👩‍👧 Fiery new look!

Lucía tiene fleco. - Lucía has bangs.
(loo-SEE-ah TYEH-neh FLEH-koh)
🔄 You can also say ***flequillo***.

Personality

Me cae muy bien. - I really like him/her.
(meh KAH-eh mooy byehn)
👩‍👩‍👧 Instant good vibes.

Miguel es simpático, ¿verdad? - Miguel is nice, isn't he?
(mee-GEHL ehs seem-PAH-tee-koh behr-DAHD)
👩‍👩‍👧 Everybody's favorite guy.

Mi prima es tímida. - My cousin is shy.
(mee PREE-mah ehs TEE-mee-dah)
👩‍👩‍👧 Quiet, but with a big heart.

Papá es muy trabajador. - Dad is very hardworking.
(pah-PAH ehs mooy trah-bah-hah-DOHR)
👨‍👩‍👧‍👦 The family hero.

Andrés es flojo. - Andrés is lazy.
(ahn-DREHS ehs FLOH-hoh)
🧑 Professional napper.

Mamá es amable. - Mom is kind.
(mah-MAH ehs ah-MAH-bleh)
👨‍👩‍👧‍👦 Always there with love.

La maestra es seria. - The teacher is serious.
(lah mah-EHS-trah ehs SEH-ryah)
👨‍👩‍👧‍👦 Better do your homework!

Juan es divertido. - Juan is fun.
(HWAHN ehs dee-behr-TEE-doh)
👨‍👩‍👧‍👦 The life of the party.

Soy bastante neurótico. - I am quite neurotic.
(soy bahs-TAHN-teh neh-oo-ROH-tee-koh)
👨‍👩‍👧‍👦 At least you're aware of it!

Mi hermano menor es enojón. - My younger brother is grumpy.
(mee ehr-MAH-noh meh-NOHR ehs eh-noh-HOHN)
🧑 The family's little grouch.

Laura es honesta. - Laura is honest.
(LAH-oo-rah ehs oh-NEHS-tah)
🧑 Straightforward and trustworthy.

Mi sobrino es curioso. - My nephew is curious.
(mee soh-BREE-noh ehs koo-RYOH-soh)
👨‍👩‍👧‍👦 Always asking "Why?".

💡 No Sabo Challenge

Do you have any family pictures of relatives you haven't met? Then go over them with an older family member and ask them to describe their personalities. Pay attention to the phrases they use and try out the ones you've learned today to describe your relatives' appearance. Record everything and then post your video on TikTok or Instagram (with the person's permission, of course) with the hashtag #NoSaboChallenge. Look up the hashtag to check out what other Latino families are like!

Chapter 12:

Pets

¿Tienes mascotas? - Do you have pets?
(TYEH-nehs mahs-KOH-tahs)
🐶 The best conversation starter for animal lovers.

¿Te gustan más los perros o los gatos? - Do you like dogs or cats more?
(teh GOOS-tahn mahs lohs PEH-rrohs oh lohs GAH-tohs)
🐶 Warning: this question may start a heated debate!

¿Tienes animales exóticos? - Do you have exotic animals?
(TYEH-nehs ah-nee-MAH-lehs ehk-SOH-tee-kohs)
🐶 Like a mini zoo at home.

Soy alérgica al pelo de conejo. - I am allergic to rabbit fur.
(soy ah-LEHR-hee-kah ahl PEH-loh deh koh-NEH-hoh)
🐶 Cute but sneezy.

¿Te gustan los conejillos de indias? - Do you like Guinea pigs?
(teh GOOS-tahn lohs koh-neh-HEE-johs deh EEN-dyahs)
🔄 This animal is also called **cobayo** or **cuy** in South America.

Tengo que desparasitar a mi perro. - I have to deworm my dog.
(TEHN-goh keh dehs-pah-rah-see-TAHR ah mee PEH-rroh)
🐶 Not glamorous, but necessary.

¿De qué raza es? - What breed is it?
(deh keh RRAH-sah ehs)
🐶 Every dog parent's favorite question.

Tiene un collar con su nombre. - It has a collar with a nametag.
(TYEH-neh oon koh-JAHR kohn soo NOHM-breh)
🐶 Stylish and safe.

Mi perro se porta bien. - My dog is well-behaved.
(mee PEH-rroh seh POHR-tah byehn)
🐶 Such a good boy!

Debo llevarlo al veterinario. - I must take him to the vet.
(DEH-boh jeh-BAHR-loh ahl beh-teh-ree-NAH-ryoh)
🐶 Health comes first!

Ayer vacuné a mi perro. - Yesterday I vaccinated my dog.
(ah-JEHR bah-koo-NEH ah mee PEH-rroh)
🐶 One less worry.

Le doy una pastilla en un trozo de queso. - I give him a pill inside a piece of cheese.
(leh DOY OO-nah pahs-TEE-jah en oon TROH-soh deh KEH-soh)
🐶 Cheese: the universal disguise.

Adopté una perra. - I adopted a female dog.
(ah-dohp-TEH OO-nah PEH-rrah)
🐶 Rescue is love.

Mi gatito nació ciego. - My kitten was born blind.
(mee gah-TEE-toh nah-SYOH SYEH-goh)
🐶 Still perfect and full of love.

Todas mis mascotas son de la perrera. - All my pets are

from the shelter.
(TOH-dahs mees mahs-KOH-tahs sohn deh lah peh-RREH-rah)

🐶 Adopt, don't buy!

Me gusta transitar animales. - I like to foster animals.
(meh GOOS-tah trahn-see-TAHR ah-nee-MAH-lehs)

🐶 Temporary homes, forever love.

Trabajo con animales de granja. - I work with farm animals.
(trah-BAH-hoh kohn ah-nee-MAH-lehs deh GRAHN-hah)

🐶 Moo, oink, cluck all day long.

Mi gato es muy arisco. - My cat is very unfriendly.
(mee GAH-toh ehs mooy ah-REES-koh)

🐶 Independent vibes only.

Mi perro es juguetón. - My dog is playful.
(mee PEH-rroh ehs hoo-geh-TOHN)

🐶 Endless energy and tail wags.

Mi hija tiene una pecera grande. - My daughter has a big fish tank.
(mee EE-hah TYEH-neh OO-nah peh-SEH-rah GRAHN-deh)
🐶 Like an underwater TV.

Saco a pasear a mi perro todos los días. - I walk my dog every day.
(SAH-koh ah pah-seh-AHR ah mee PEH-rroh TOH-dohs lohs DEE-ahs)
🐶 Best exercise buddy ever.

Max es un perro de servicio. - Max is a service dog.
(MAX ehs oon PEH-rroh deh sehr-BEE-syoh)
🐶 A true hero on four paws.

Es ilegal tener tortugas de mascota aquí. - It's illegal to have turtles as pets here.
(ehs ee-leh-GAHL teh-NEHR tohr-TOO-gahs deh mahs-KOH-tah ah-KEE)
🐶 Sorry, Ninja Turtles fans.

Castramos a mi gata el mes pasado. - We spayed my cat last month.
(kahs-TRAH-mohs ah mee GAH-tah ehl mehs pah-SAH-doh)
🐶 Responsible pet parenting.

Mi tía tiene un loro que habla. - My aunt has a talking parrot.
(mee TEE-ah TYEH-neh oon LOH-roh keh AH-blah)
🐶 The family gossip parrot.

Mi cachorro hizo pis en la alfombra. - My puppy peed on the carpet.
(mee kah-CHOH-rroh EE-soh pees ehn lah al-FOHM-brah)
🐶 Oops... puppy training in progress.

No me gustan los animales. - I don't like animals.
(no meh GOOS-tahn lohs ah-nee-MAH-lehs)
🐶 That's okay, more pets for the rest of us!

Between Cultures: In Mexico and other Latin American countries, it's common to find an exotic pet called *ajolote* or *axolótl*. It's a type of aquatic salamander with gills! This animal is named after the Aztec deity Xolotl, the god of fire and lightning. *Axólotl* also means water monster in the Nahuatl language. The Argentinian writer Julio Cortázar wrote an amazing short story titled "Axolótl".

💡 No Sabo Challenge:

Do you have any pets? Record them and say phrases about them in Spanish by using the content you learned! Then, post your video on TikTok or Instagram with the hashtag #NoSaboChallenge. Look up the hashtag to see other Latino pets!

Chapter 13:

Untranslatable Idioms

Estar papando moscas. - To be daydreaming.
(ehs-TAHR pah-PAHN-doh MOHS-kahs)
🤔 Watch out, reality is calling!

Estar al horno. - To be in trouble.
(ehs-TAHR ahl OHR-noh)
🤔 Things are heating up... literally. If you're really in a twist you can add ***con papas*** (with fries).

Si te digo, te miento. - If I tell you, I'd be lying.
(see teh DEE-goh, teh MYEHN-toh)
🤔 Secrets, secrets!

No tener pelos en la lengua. - To be blunt / speak your mind.
(noh teh-NEHR PEH-lohs ehn lah LEN-gwah)
🤔 No sugarcoating here.

Le faltan un par de jugadores. - He/she's not very sharp.
(leh FAHL-tahn oon pahr deh hoo-gah-DOH-rehs)
🔄 In Argentina (all football fans), say this phrase a lot: "He/she is missing a few players". You might also hear ***No le llega agua al tanque*** ("no water is reaching his/her tank").

Se armó la gorda. - All hell broke loose.
(seh ahr-MOH lah GOHR-dah)
🤔 Chaos incoming!

Meter la pata. - To mess up.
(meh-TEHR lah PAH-tah)
😬 Oops... did I just say that?

Se le subieron los humos. - He/she is being cocky.
(seh leh soo-BYEH-ron lohs OO-mohs)
🌐 When someone is being arrogant we say that "The fumes have gone up to their head".

Estar como agua para el chocolate. - To be really mad.
(ehs-TAHR KOH-moh AH-gwah PAH-rah ehl choh-koh-LAH-teh)
🌐 You will probably hear this phrase in Mexico. The water needs to be close to boiling if you want to make hot chocolate!

Estar hasta las manos. - Deeply infatuated / in over your head.
(ehs-TAHR AHS-tah lahs MAH-nohs)
🌐 This phrase literally means "To be up to your hands" and is mainly used in Argentina and Uruguay.

Estar en la luna. - To be daydreaming.
(ehs-TAHR ehn lah LOO-nah)
🌐 You can also say ***Estar en Babia***.

Costar un ojo de la cara. - To cost an arm and a leg.
(kohs-TAHR oon OH-hoh deh lah KAH-rah)
😬 Different body parts, but still pricey!

Quedar de piedra. - To be stunned / shocked.
(keh-DAHR deh PYEH-drah)
😬 Speechless!

Ser uña y carne. - Like two peas in a pod.
(sehr OO-nyah ee KAHR-neh)
🌐 You can also say ***Ser uña y mugre*** ("dirt").

Estar hecho/hecha polvo. - To be exhausted / worn out.
(es-TAHR EH-choh/EH-chah POHL-boh)
🫠 I need a nap... or a vacation.

Írsele la mano. - To go too far / lose control.
(EER-seh-leh lah MAH-noh)
🫠 Oops... maybe too much.

Cabeza de chorlito. - Scatterbrain.
(kah-BEH-sah deh chor-LEE-toh)
🫠 Someone is always losing their keys!

Between Cultures: Saying that these idioms are "untranslatable" also works the other way around. A lot of English phrases don't make any sense when translating them into Spanish, like **hit the books** or **bite the bullet**.

💡 No Sabo Challenge

Go talk to a Spanish-speaking relative and make them explain the literal meaning of these Spanish phrases we've taught you! You can do the opposite joke with some untranslatable English phrases. Then, post your video on TikTok or Instagram (with the person's permission, of course) with the hashtag #NoSaboChallenge! Look up the hashtag to see other fun phrases.

Chapter 14:

Hobbies

Cinema and TV

Miro una película. - I watch a movie.
(MEE-roh OO-nah peh-LEE-koo-lah)
🎨 Popcorn required.

Soy cinéfilo/cinéfila. - I am a movie lover.
(soy see-NEH-fee-loh/see-NEH-fee-lah)
🎨 Netflix is basically your soulmate.

¿Has visto alguna buena película últimamente? - Have you seen any good movies lately?
(ahs BEES-toh al-GOO-nah BWEH-nah peh-LEE-koo-lah ool-tee-mah-MEHN-teh)
🎨 Classic small talk.

¿Te gustan las comedias románticas? - Do you like romantic comedies?
(teh GOOS-tahn lahs koh-MEH-dyahs roh-MAHN-tee-kahs)
🎨 Love, laughs, and popcorn.

¿Te gustan las películas de terror? - Do you like horror movies?
(teh GOOS-tahn lahs peh-LEE-koo-lahs deh teh-RROHR)
🎨 Don't forget to cover your eyes.

¿Cuál es tu personaje favorito? - Who is your favorite character?

(kwahl ehs too pehr-soh-NAH-heh fah-boh-REE-toh)
🎨 Everyone has a favorite hero.

¿Qué te pareció el final de la serie? - What did you think of the series finale?
(keh teh pah-reh-SYOH ehl fee-NAHL deh lah SEH-ryeh)
🎨 Warning: spoiler alert.

¿Ya viste el final de temporada? - Did you already see the season finale?
(jah BEES-teh ehl fee-NAHL deh tehm-poh-RAH-dah)
🎨 Binge-watchers know the struggle.

Me spoilearon el final de la peli. - They spoiled the ending for me.
(meh spoy-leh-AH-rohn ehl fee-NAHL deh lah PEH-lee)
✏️ It's common to use the short version **peli** instead of *película*.

La primera temporada es la mejor. - The first season is the best.
(lah pree-MEH-rah tehm-poh-RAH-dah ehs lah meh-HOHR)
🎨 Nothing beats the beginning.

No entendí el final... - I didn't understand the ending...
(noh ehn-tehn-DEE ehl fee-NAHL)
🎨 You're not alone!

Esta película está basada en un caso real. - This movie is based on a true story.
(EHS-tah peh-LEE-koo-lah ehs-TAH bah-SAH-dah en oon KAH-soh reh-AHL)
🎨 Even scarier than fiction.

Es una película muy pretenciosa. - It's a very pretentious movie.
(ehs OO-nah peh-LEE-koo-lah mooy preh-ten-SYOH-sah)
🎨 The artsy vibes are strong.

¡Interstellar está sobrevalorada! - Interstellar is overrated!
(een-tehr-STEH-lahr ehs-TAH soh-breh-bah-loh-RAH-dah)
🎨 Controversial opinion alert.

No miro películas con subtítulos. - I don't watch movies with subtitles.
(noh MEE-roh peh-LEE-koo-lahs kohn soob-TEE-too-lohs)
🎨 You're missing out!

Hay un festival de cine francés. - There's a French film festival.
(AH-y oon fehs-tee-BAHL deh SEE-neh frahn-SEHS)
🎨 *Bonjour, cinéma!*

Los diálogos son poco creíbles. - The dialogues are not very believable.
(lohs dee-AH-loh-gohs sohn POH-koh kreh-EE-blehs)
🎨 Nobody talks like that in real life.

Él es un pésimo actor. - He is a terrible actor.
(ehl ehs oon PEH-see-moh ahk-TOHR)
🎨 Ouch... harsh but true.

La banda sonora es excelente. - The soundtrack is excellent.
(lah BAHN-dah soh-NOH-rah ehs ehk-seh-LEHN-teh)
🎨 Music makes the magic.

Me encantan las series de época. - I love period dramas.
(meh en-KAHN-tahn lahs SEH-ryehs deh EH-poh-kah)
🎨 Corsets and castles, please.

La premisa es muy original. - The premise is very original.
(lah preh-MEE-sah ehs mooy oh-ree-hee-NAHL)
🎨 Fresh stories are the best.

La trama era demasiado compleja. - The plot was too complex.

(lah TRAH-mah EH-rah deh-mah-SYAH-doh kom-PLEH-hah)
🎨 Wait, what just happened?

Between Cultures: Latin American culture isn't as work-focused as US culture. For instance, people's jobs aren't the only topic of conversation (and sometimes your job won't come up at all!): we enjoy talking about our hobbies and the things we love to do.

Sports

¿Qué deporte te gusta? - What sport do you like?
(keh deh-POHR-teh teh GOOS-tah)
🎨 The icebreaker question.

¿Viste el partido de ayer? - Did you watch yesterday's game?
(BEES-teh ehl pahr-TEE-doh deh ah-YEHR)
🎨 Always a hot topic.

¡Qué mal juegan! - They play so badly!
(keh mahl HWEH-gahn)
🎨 The eternal fan frustration.

Messi es el mejor jugador del mundo. - Messi is the best player in the world.
(MEH-see ehs ehl meh-HOHR hoo-gah-DOHR del MOON-doh)
🎨 The GOAT.

¿Jugamos un partido? - Shall we play a match?
(hoo-GAH-mohs oon pahr-TEE-doh)
🎨 Time to lace up your shoes.

¿Juegas al básquetbol? - Do you play basketball?
(HWEH-gahs ahl BAHS-keht-bohl)

117

🎨 You can also say **baloncesto** or **básket**.

¿Te gusta el tenis? - Do you like tennis?
(teh GOOS-tah ehl TEH-nees)
🎨 Game, set, match.

El béisbol es demasiado largo para mí. - Baseball is too long for me.
(ehl BEHYS-bohl ehs deh-mah-SYAH-doh LAHR-goh PAH-rah mee)
🎨 Too many innings, not enough patience.

¿Vamos al partido? - Shall we go to the game?
(BAH-mohs ahl pahr-TEE-doh)
🌐 In South America, people say **Vamos a la cancha** (*cancha* is the field).

Creo que ganarán 2 a 1. - I think they will win 2 to 1.
(KREH-oh keh gah-nah-RAHN DOHS ah OO-noh)
🎨 Sports predictions are always risky.

El partido terminó en empate. - The match ended in a tie.
(ehl pahr-TEE-doh tehr-mee-NOH ehn em-PAH-teh)
🎨 Nobody wins, nobody loses.

¿Habrá penales? - Will there be penalties?
(ah-BRAH peh-NAH-lehs)
🎨 The most stressful moment.

Desde aquí no puedo ver la pelota. - From here I can't see the ball.
(DEHS-deh ah-KEE noh PWEH-doh behr lah peh-LOH-tah)
🎨 Should've brought binoculars.

¿Quieres jugar? - Do you want to play?
(KYEH-rehs hoo-GAHR)

🎨 Simple and fun.

¿Juegas competitivo? - Do you play competitively?
(HWEH-gahs kohm-peh-tee-TEE-boh)
🎨 If you're part of a club, you are a **deportista federado** (an athlete recognized by an official sports federation).

Videogames

Salió un nuevo juego de mundo abierto. - A new open-world game just came out.
(sah-LYOH oon NWEH-boh HWEH-goh deh MOON-doh ah-BYEHR-toh)
🎨 Goodbye, social life.

Prefiero los RPG. - I prefer RPGs.
(preh-FYEH-roh lohs EH-rreh peh heh)
✏️ You have to pronounce the letters in Spanish!

¿Jugamos una partida? - Shall we play a match?
(hoo-GAH-mohs OO-nah pahr-TEE-dah)
🎨 Grab your controller!

Ponle pausa. - Pause it.
(POHN-leh PAH-oo-sah)
🎨 Break time.

Debemos ganarle al jefe. - We have to beat the boss.
(deh-BEH-mohs gah-NAHR-leh ahl HEH-feh)
🎨 Final battle time!

Espera, ya me conecto. - Wait, I'm logging in now.
(ehs-PEH-rah jah meh koh-NEHK-toh)
🎨 Gaming friends unite.

Tengo lag. - I have lag.
(TEHN-goh lag)
🎨 A gamer's worst nightmare.

El Internet me está funcionando mal. - The Internet is not working well for me.
(ehl een-tehr-NEHT meh ehs-TAH foon-syoh-NAHN-doh mahl)
🎨 Wi-Fi, don't betray me!

Creí que ganaríamos. - I thought we would win.
(kreh-EE keh gah-nah-REE-ah-mohs)
🎨 Defeat hurts.

Soy el MVP. / Salí MVP. - I am the MVP.
(soy ehl ehm bee pee / sah-LEE ehm bee pee)
✏️ In this case, the acronym is pronounced just like in English.

Music

¿Qué tipo de música escuchas? - What type of music do you listen to?
(keh TEE-poh deh MOO-see-kah ehs-KOO-chahs)
🎨 The ultimate taste reveal.

A mí me gusta el rock. - I like rock.
(ah mee meh GOOS-tah ehl rock)
🎨 Rock on!

¿Has escuchado el último álbum de Morat? - Have you listened to Morat's latest album?
(ahs ehs-koo-CHAH-doh ehl OOL-tee-moh AHL-boom deh moh-RAHT)
🎨 Fan moment incoming.

Me ha encantado la última canción que lanzó. - I loved the

last song they released.
(meh ah ehn-kahn-TAH-doh lah OOL-tee-mah kahn-SYOHN keh lahn-SOH)
🎨 On repeat all day.

¿Cuál es tu artista preferido? - Who is your favorite artist?
(kwahl ehs too ahr-TEES-tah preh-feh-REE-doh)
🎨 Hardest question ever.

Esa canción es muy pegadiza. - That song is very catchy.
(EH-sah kahn-SYOHN ehs mooy peh-gah-DEE-sah)
🎨 Stuck in your head forever.

Se me pegó la última canción de Shakira. - Shakira's last song got stuck in my head.
(seh meh peh-GOH lah OOL-tee-mah kahn-SYOHN deh shah-KEE-rah)
🎨 Hips don't lie, neither do catchy songs.

¿Tocas algún instrumento? - Do you play an instrument?
(TOH-kahs ahl-GOON een-stroo-MEHN-toh)
🎨 Future rockstar maybe?

¿Qué música escuchas? - What music do you listen to?
(keh MOO-see-kah ehs-KOO-chahs)
🎨 Music tells your story.

¿Te gusta bailar salsa? - Do you like salsa dancing?
(teh GOOS-tah bah-ee-LAHR SAHL-sah)
🎨 Time to move your hips!

Empecé a tomar clases de bachata. - I started taking bachata lessons.
(ehm-peh-SEH ah toh-MAHR KLAH-sehs deh bah-CHAH-tah)
🎨 Smooth moves incoming.

Me encanta el pop latino. - I love Latin pop.
(meh ehn-KAHN-tah ehl pop lah-TEE-noh)
🎨 Catchy and fun.

Estoy aprendiendo a tocar el piano. - I am learning to play the piano.
(ehs-TOY ah-prehn-DYEHN-doh ah toh-KAHR ehl PYAH-noh)
🎨 Future pianist in the making.

Libros

¿Te gusta leer? - Do you like to read?
(teh GOOS-tah leh-EHR)
🎨 The classic bookworm question.

¿Me recomiendas un libro? - Can you recommend me a book?
(meh reh-koh-MYEHN-dahs oon LEE-broh)
🎨 Book recs are the best.

¿Has leído algo bueno últimamente? - Have you read anything good lately?
(ahs leh-EE-doh AHL-goh BWEH-noh ool-tee-mah-MEHN-teh)
🎨 Readers love this one.

Me gusta la ciencia ficción. - I like science fiction.
(meh GOOS-tah lah SYEHN-syah feek-SYOHN)
🎨 To infinity and beyond!

¿De qué se trata la historia? - What is the story about?
(deh keh seh TRAH-tah lah ehs-TOH-ryah)
🎨 Spoiler-free answers, please.

¿Cuál es tu autor favorito? - Who is your favorite author?

(kwahl ehs too ah-oo-TOHR fah-boh-REE-toh)
🎨 Impossible to choose just one.

¿Tienes una novela preferida? - Do you have a favorite novel?
(TYEH-nehs OO-nah noh-BEH-lah preh-feh-REE-dah)
🎨 The one you'd reread forever.

Me cuesta leer poesía. - I find it hard to read poetry.
(meh KWEHS-tah leh-EHR poh-eh-SEE-ah)
🎨 It's not for everyone, and that's okay.

Ella ganó el premio Nobel de Literatura. - She won the Nobel Prize in Literature.
(EH-jah gah-NOH ehl PREH-myoh NOH-bel deh lee-teh-rah-TOO-rah)
🎨 A true literary star.

Es un escritor poco conocido. - He is a little-known writer.
(ehs oon ehs-kree-TOHR POH-koh koh-noh-SEE-doh)
🎨 Hidden gem alert.

Me encantan los cuentos policiales. - I love detective stories.
(meh ehn-KAHN-tahn lohs KWEHN-tohs poh-lee-SYAH-lehs)
🎨 Sherlock Holmes vibes.

¿Qué tipo de libros te gustan? - What kind of books do you like?
(keh TEE-poh deh LEE-brohs teh GOOS-tahn)
🎨 The ultimate book question.

¿Cuántos libros lees al año? - How many books do you read per year?
(KWAHN-tohs LEE-brohs LEH-ehs ahl AH-nyoh)
🎨 Bragging rights unlocked.

¿Prefieres libros electrónicos o de papel? - Do you prefer e-books or paper books?
(preh-FYEH-rehs LEE-brohs eh-lehk-TROH-nee-kohs oh deh pah-PEHL)
🎨 Team Kindle vs. Team Paper.

Harán una película sobre ese fan fiction. - They're making a movie about that fan fiction.
(ah-RAHN OO-nah peh-LEE-koo-lah SOH-breh EH-seh fahn FEEK-shohn)
🎨 From fandom to the big screen!

💡 No Sabo Challenge

Do you practice any hobbies? Film yourself as you do them and say some of the Spanish phrases you've learned today. Then, post your video on TikTok or Instagram with the hashtag #NoSaboChallenge! Look up the hashtag to check out what other hobbies are called in Spanish!

Chapter 15:

School & Education

¿Cómo te fue en la escuela? - How was school?
(KOH-moh teh fweh ehn lah ehs-KWEH-lah)
🏫 The daily check-in.

¿Cuál es tu asignatura favorita? - What is your favorite subject?
(kwahl ehs too ah-seeg-nah-TOO-rah fah-boh-REE-tah)
🏫 Math? History? Lunch?

¿Cómo se llama tu profesora? - What is your teacher's name?
(KOH-moh seh JAH-mah too proh-feh-SOH-rah)
🏫 Always good to know!

¿Eres bueno/buena en matemáticas? - Are you good at math?
(EH-rehs BWEH-noh/BWEH-nah en mah-teh-MAH-tee-kahs)
🏫 Numbers don't lie... but sometimes we wish they did.

¿Te gustan las Ciencias Sociales? - Do you like Social Studies?
(teh GOOS-tahn lahs SYEHN-syahs soh-SYAH-lehs)
🏫 Maps, history, and debates galore.

Me cuesta mucho Física. - I find Physics very hard.
(meh KWEHS-tah MOO-choh FEE-see-kah)
🏫 Gravity always pulling us down.

¿Cómo te fue en el examen? - How did the exam go?
(KOH-moh teh fweh ehn ehl ehk-SAH-mehn)
🏫 The million-dollar question.

¿Hiciste la tarea? - Did you do your homework?
(ee-SEES-teh lah tah-REH-ah)
🔄 You can also say **los deberes**.

Pasé con siete. - I passed with a seven.
(pah-SEH kohn SYEH-teh)
🏮 Not bad, not bad at all!

Between Cultures: In Latin America, most schools use numbers instead of letters to grade students, and the maximum scores change depending on the country:

● Argentina / Mexico → 1-10, passing is usually 4 (Argentina) or 6 (Mexico).

● Venezuela / Peru → 0-20, passing is 10 (Venezuela) or 11 (Peru).

● Chile → 1.0-7.0, passing is 4.0.

● Colombia → 0.0-5.0, passing is 3.0.

Reprobé el examen de Literatura. - I failed the Literature exam.
(reh-proh-BEH ehl ehk-SAH-men deh lee-teh-rah-TOO-rah)
🏮 If only you'd read the novel!

Tengo un trabajo práctico grupal. - I have a group project.
(TEHN-goh oon trah-BAH-hoh PRAHK-tee-koh groo-PAHL)
🏮 Pray for good teammates.

Necesito estudiar para la prueba. - I need to study for the test.
(neh-seh-SEE-toh ehs-too-DYAHR PAH-rah lah PRWEH-bah)
🏮 Coffee, books, repeat.

Mi maestro me tiene de punto. - My teacher has it in for me.
(mee mah-EHS-troh meh TYEH-neh deh POON-toh)
🏛 Feels like they've got a radar on you.

La profe sustituta es muy estricta. - The substitute teacher is very strict.
(lah PROH-feh soos-tee-TOO-tah ehs mooy ehs-TREEK-tah)
🔄 You can also say ***profesor/a suplente***.

¿Irás a la fiesta de graduación? - Are you going to the graduation party?
(ee-RAHS ah lah FYEHS-tah deh grah-dwah-SYOHN)
🔄 In Argentina, it's called ***fiesta de egresados***.

¿Quién es tu compañero/compañera de banco? - Who is your desk mate?
(kyehn ehs too kohm-pah-NYEH-roh/kohm-pah-NYEH-rah deh BAHN-koh)
🏛 Friend... or distraction?

Saquen una hoja. - Take out a sheet of paper.
(SAH-kehn OO-nah OH-hah)
🏛 Uh-oh... surprise quiz incoming.

Odio los exámenes orales. - I hate oral exams.
(OH-dyoh lohs ehk-SAH-meh-nehs oh-RAH-lehs)
🏛 The anxiety is real.

Hicimos un repaso la clase anterior al examen. - We did a review the class before the exam.
(ee-SEE-mohs oon reh-PAH-soh lah KLAH-seh ahn-teh-RYO-HR ahl ehk-SAH-mehn)
🏛 Last-minute saving grace.

Hoy tuvimos prueba sorpresa. - Today we had a surprise test.

(oy too-BEE-mohs PRWEH-bah sohr-PREH-sah)
🏫 The worst surprise ever.

¿Ya sabes qué vas a estudiar cuando termines? - Do you already know what you will study when you finish?
(jah SAH-behs keh bahs ah ehs-too-DYAHR KWAHN-doh tehr-MEE-nehs)
🏫 The big life question.

Ayer me enviaron a dirección. - Yesterday they sent me to the principal's office.
(ah-JEHR meh ehn-BYAH-rohn ah dee-rehk-SYOHN)
🔄 You can also say **a la oficina del director/de la directora.**

Me suspendieron por una semana. - I was suspended for a week.
(meh soos-pehn-DYEH-rohn pohr OO-nah seh-MAH-nah)
🏫 Extra vacation?

Mi parte preferida de la escuela es el recreo. - My favorite part of school is recess.
(mee PAHR-teh preh-feh-REE-dah deh lah ehs-KWEH-lah ehs ehl reh-KREH-oh)
🏫 Snack time forever.

Dejo los libros en mi casillero. - I leave my books in my locker.
(DEH-hoh lohs LEE-brohs en mee kah-see-JEH-roh)
🏫 Smart move to save your back.

¿Cómo te fue en el SAT? - How did you do on the SAT?
(KOH-moh teh fweh ehn ehl ehs-ey-TEE)
✏️ "SAT" is pronounced in the English way!

Soy el mejor promedio de mi clase. - I am the top student in my class.

(soy ehl meh-HOHR proh-MEH-dyoh deh mee KLAH-seh)
 Brains and bragging rights.

💡 No Sabo Challenge

Are you still in school or studying at college? Record yourself inside campus (respectfully, not using your phone in class) and use some of the Spanish phrases you've learned today to describe your education experience. Then, post your video on TikTok or Instagram with the hashtag #NoSaboChallenge! Look up the hashtag to check what other students are doing!

Chapter 16:

Body & Health

Illnesses and Pains

Me duele la cabeza. - My head hurts.
(meh DWEH-leh lah kah-BEH-sah)
🖌 Classic excuse to skip family *chisme* hour—works every time.

Tengo fiebre. - I have a fever.
(TEHN-goh FYEH-breh)
🖌 Say it and abuela will instantly bring you Vick VapoRub
(pronounced *beek bah-poh-ROO* by most Latinos).

Tengo tos. - I have a cough.
(TEHN-goh tohs)
🖌 You can change *tos* for other symptoms as well, even
Tengo dolor de cabeza.

Tengo dolor de espalda. - I have back pain.
(TEHN-goh doh-LOHR deh ehs-PAHL-dah)
🖌 Perfect for avoiding moving furniture at family gatherings.

Me doblé el tobillo. - I twisted my ankle.
(meh doh-BLEH ehl toh-BEE-joh)
🖌 Bonus drama if you limp a little—instant sympathy points.

Me quebré la pierna. - I broke my leg.
(meh keh-BREH lah PYER-nah)

✏️ You can change *la pierna* with other parts of the body, of course!

Me operé la rodilla. - I had knee surgery.
(meh oh-peh-REH lah rroh-DEE-jah)
✏️ Change rodilla for ***cadera*** (hip) or ***hombro*** (shoulder) to cover other classic surgery spots.

Me esguincé la muñeca. - I sprained my wrist.
(meh ehs-geen-SEH lah moo-NYEH-kah)
✏️ Extra dramatic if you wrap it with a huge bandage.

Estoy resfriado/resfriada. - I have a cold.
(ehs-TOY res-free-AH-doh/res-free-AH-dah)
🔄 In México they say ***Tengo gripa***, in Puerto Rico, ***Estoy acatarrado***.

Me bajó la presión. - My blood pressure dropped.
(meh bah-HOH lah preh-SYOHN)
✏️ You can also flip it to ***Me subió la presión***—both get you instant *abuela* attention.

Soy diabético/diabética. - I'm diabetic.
(soy dyah-BEH-tee-koh/dyah-BEH-tee-kah)
✏️ Useful when *tía* insists on giving you *tres leches* cake.

Between Cultures: In the US, health care is often private and expensive, with insurance playing a big role in access. Preventive care and fitness culture are common, but costs can be a barrier. In Latin America, public health systems exist in most countries, though quality varies. Many people mix public hospitals, private clinics, and home remedies. Family traditions are still part of daily health practices.

Key Health Questions

¿Has tomado algo para el dolor? - Have you taken anything for the pain?
(ahs toh-MAH-doh AHL-goh PAH-rah ehl doh-LOHR)
🪶 Sounds like a doctor, but also like a nosy cousin.

¿Qué te duele? - What hurts?
(keh teh DWEH-leh)
🔄 Answer with any body part: *la espalda*, *los ojos*, *la garganta*. Endless combos.

¿Quieres ir al doctor? - Do you want to go to the doctor?
(KYEH-rehs eer ahl dohk-TOHR)
🪶 Usually said by mom when things are serious—or not at all.

Vamos a la sala de emergencias. - Let's go to the ER.
(BAH-mohs ah lah SAH-lah deh eh-mehr-HEHN-syahs)
🪶 You'll hear this once mom is done trying home remedies.

¿Fuiste al hospital? - Did you go to the hospital?
(FWEES-teh ahl ohs-pee-TAHL)
🪶 Swap *hospital* for **clínica** to fit local wording in many countries.

Estás pálido/pálida. - You look pale.
(ehs-TAHS PAH-lee-doh/PAH-lee-dah)
🪶 *Tías* love saying this right before serving more food.

Tienes mala pinta. - You don't look well.
(TYEH-nehs MAH-lah PEEN-tah)
🔄 In Venezuela they say **Tienes mala cara**, in México **Te ves mal**.

At the Doctor's Office

Te haremos unos estudios. - We'll run some tests.
(teh ah-REH-mohs OO-nohs ehs-TOO-dyohs)
🗨 You may also hear ***Te haremos unos exámenes***—same meaning.

Te haremos un análisis de sangre. - We'll do a blood test.
(teh ah-REH-mohs oon ah-NAH-lee-sees deh SAHN-greh)
🗨 Swap *sangre* for **orina** ("urine") or **saliva**—more vocab and less scary.

Te tomaré la presión. - I'll take your blood pressure.
(teh toh-mah-REH lah preh-SYOHN)
🔄 You can also hear ***Te mediré la presión*** in many countries.

¿Puedes respirar profundo? - Can you take a deep breath?
(PWEH-dehs rres-pee-RAHR proh-FOON-doh)
🗨 It also works for anxiety before exams.

Toma este medicamento por 3 días. - Take this medicine for 3 days.
(TOH-mah EHS-teh meh-dee-kah-MEHN-toh pohr trehs DEE-ahs)
🗨 Depending on what you have, *3 días* may be **una semana** or more.

Debes descansar. - You should rest.
(DEH-behs dehs-kahn-SAHR)
🗨 Latin family for: "Stay in bed while we bring you soup."

Debes hacer reposo. - You should take bed rest.
(DEH-behs ah-SEHR reh-POH-soh)
🔄 Alternative phrasing: ***Debes quedarte en cama.***

Accidents, Emergencies and Natural Disasters

Hubo un choque en la carretera. - There was a crash on the highway.
(OO-boh oon CHOH-keh ehn lah kah-rreh-TEH-rah)
🚀 This may lead to a good *chisme* or may cause *preocupación*.

Me robaron el coche. - They stole my car.
(meh rroh-BAH-rohn ehl KOH-cheh)
🔄 In México they say **carro**, in Argentina **auto**.

Me arrebataron el bolso. - They snatched my purse.
(meh ah-rreh-bah-TAH-rohn ehl BOHL-soh)
🔄 In México **bolsa**, in Colombia and South America, **cartera** (but in Spain it means "wallet").

Entraron a mi casa. - They broke into my house.
(ehn-TRAH-rohn ah mee KAH-sah)
🚀 The nightmare phrase nobody wants to use.

No encuentro mi cartera. - I can't find my wallet.
(noh ehn-KWEHN-troh mee kar-TEH-rah)
🔄 In many Latin American countries, we say **billetera**.

Me caí por las escaleras. - I fell down the stairs.
(meh kah-EE pohr lahs ehs-kah-LEH-rahs)
🚀 Always comes with a dramatic re-enactment.

Estuve en una pelea. - I was in a fight.
(ehs-TOO-beh ehn OO-nah peh-LEH-ah)
🚀 Guarantees instant family *chisme*.

¡Esa casa está en llamas! - That house is on fire!
(EH-sah KAH-sah ehs-TAH ehn JAH-mahs)
🚀 Cue the action-movie soundtrack.

Hay un incendio forestal. - There's a forest fire.
(AH-y oon een-SEHN-dyoh foh-rehs-TAHL)
🖊 Sadly, a way too common phrase during the summer.

Un tornado destruyó mi pueblo. - A tornado destroyed my town.
(oon tohr-NAH-doh dehs-troo-JOH mee PWEH-bloh)
🖊 It may be something other than a *tornado*, of course, like **una inundación** (" a flood").

El huracán Katrina fue muy fuerte. - Hurricane Katrina was very strong.
(ehl oo-rah-KAHN kah-TREE-nah fweh MOO-y FWEHR-teh)
🖊 You can use this phrase to tell your *tía* about the latest hurricane you've experienced.

El volcán erupcionó. - The volcano erupted.
(ehl bohl-KAHN eh-roop-syoh-NOH)
🖊 Not too common, but possible.

¡Una avalancha de nieve! - An avalanche!
(OO-nah ah-bah-LAHN-chah deh NYEH-beh)
🖊 In case you're traveling near the *Cordillera de los Andes*.

En 2002 hubo una gran inundación. - In 2002 there was a big flood.
(ehn dohs meel dohs OO-boh OO-nah grahn een-oon-dah-SYOHN)
🖊 Floods can be way too common in some places, still.

Es un terremoto de magnitud 5. - It's a magnitude 5 earthquake.
(ehs oon teh-rreh-MOH-toh deh mag-nee-TOOD seen-koh)
🖊 This always comes up when talking about earthquakes.

La sequía arruinó las cosechas. - The drought ruined the crops.

(lah seh-KEE-ah ah-rwee-NOH lahs koh-SEH-chahs)

✏️ This is particularly used in the countryside, but may also be used as small talk at the grocery store.

En Perú hubo alerta de tsunami. - In Peru there was a tsunami alert.
(ehn peh-ROO OO-boh ah-LEHR-tah deh soo-NAH-mee)

✏️ Contact your Peruvian relatives right away to see if everything is okay.

💡 No Sabo Challenge

Are you visiting your *abuelos*? Tell them that you're not feeling well and see how they react! It's classic *abuelos* behavior to give you all kinds of recommendations, offer food, tell you what you're doing wrong in life and get worried, all at the same time. Try it out and film their reaction. Then upload your video to TikTok or Instagram with the hashtag #NoSaboChallenge. Visit the hashtag later to show your *abuelos* how other people's *abuelos* reacted too!

Chapter 17:

Household Chores

Chores

Haz tu cama. - Make your bed.
(ahs too KAH-mah)
🔄 In countries that use *vos*, the phrase would be **Hacé tu cama**.

Cambia tus sábanas. - Change your sheets.
(KAHM-byah toos SAH-bah-nahs)
🏠 Fresh sheets = better dreams.

Pon la mesa. - Set the table.
(pohn lah MEH-sah)
🏠 You're one step closer to dinner.

Quita de la mesa. - Clear the table.
(KEE-tah deh lah MEH-sah)
🏠 Everyone's favorite part... not.

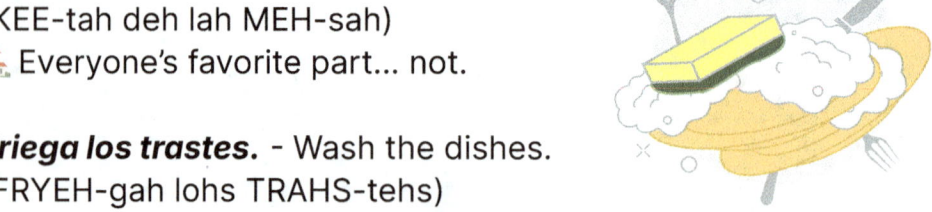

Friega los trastes. - Wash the dishes.
(FRYEH-gah lohs TRAHS-tehs)
🔄 You can also say **Lava los platos**.

Guarda los trastes secos. - Put away the dry dishes.
(GWAHR-dah lohs TRAHS-tehs SEH-kohs)
🏠 Teamwork makes the kitchen shine!

Dale de comer al gato. - Feed the cat.
(DAH-leh deh koh-MEHR ahl GAH-toh)
🏠 Otherwise, the cat will never forgive you.

Saca a pasear al perro. - Walk the dog.
(SAH-kah ah pah-seh-AHR ahl PEH-rroh)
🏠 Best exercise and therapy ever!

Ordena tu cuarto. - Tidy your room.
(ohr-DEH-nah too KWAHR-toh)
🏠 Messy room, messy mind!

Guarda tus juguetes. - Put away your toys.
(GWAHR-dah toos hoo-GEH-tehs)
🏠 So you can play again tomorrow.

Pon las cosas en su sitio. - Put things in their place.
(pohn lahs KOH-sahs ehn soo SEE-tyoh)
🏠 Chaos is not a vibe.

Friega el suelo. - Mop the floor.
(FRYEH-gah ehl SWEH-loh)
🏠 Shiny floors = happy parents.

Barre la cocina. - Sweep the kitchen.
(BAH-rreh lah koh-SEE-nah)
🏠 Crumbs don't belong there forever.

Pasa la aspiradora. - Vacuum.
(PAH-sah lah ahs-pee-rah-DOH-rah)
🏠 Say goodbye to dust bunnies.

Pon la ropa sucia en el canasto. - Put the dirty clothes in the basket.
(pohn lah RROH-pah SOO-syah ehn ehl kah-NAHS-toh)
🏠 Step one to not smelling funny.

Pon la lavadora. - Start the washing machine.
(pohn lah lah-bah-DOH-rah)
🔄 This machine is also called **el lavarropas**.

Pon la secadora. - Start the dryer.
(pohn lah seh-kah-DOH-rah)
🔄 This machine is also called **el secarropas**.

Cuelga la ropa. - Hang the clothes.
(KWEHL-gah lah RROH-pah)
🏠 Fresh air makes them smell amazing.

Plancha la ropa. - Iron the clothes.
(PLAHN-chah lah RROH-pah)
🏠 Wrinkle-free is the new chic.

Guarda la ropa. - Put away the clothes.
(GWAHR-dah lah RROH-pah)
🏠 Closet > floor, always.

Riega las plantas. - Water the plants.
(RRYEH-gah lahs PLAHN-tahs)
🏠 They're thirsty little friends.

Limpia el excusado. - Clean the toilet.
(LEEM-pyah ehl ehks-koo-SAH-doh)
🔄 This object is also called **inodoro** or **váter**.

Cambia la bombilla. - Change the light bulb.
(KAHM-byah lah bohm-BEE-jah)
🔄 You can also say **lamparita** or **foco**.

Ve a comprar leche. - Go buy milk.
(beh ah kohm-PRAHR LEH-cheh)
🏠 Don't come back with just cookies.

Between Cultures: In many Latino households, *la chancla* ("flip-flop") is a humorous yet strong form of discipline. The mere gesture of a mom picking it up can be enough to straighten behavior—no actual *chanclazo* (a flip-flop throw) needed. But jokes aside, relying on fear or physical threat can be a harmful practice for children.

Orders From Your *Mamá*

Apaga la luz. - Turn off the light.
(ah-PAH-gah lah LOOS)
🏠 Save money, save the planet.

Quítate los zapatos. - Take off your shoes.
(KEE-tah-teh lohs sah-PAH-tohs)
🏠 Your floor will thank you.

Ven aquí. - Come here.
(behn ah-KEE)
🏠 Not scary, just urgent!

Levántate, que estamos tarde. - Get up, we're late.
(leh-BAHN-tah-teh keh ehs-TAH-mohs TAHR-deh)
🏠 The snooze button betrayed you.

Silencio. - Silence.
(see-LEHN-syoh)
🏠 Sometimes golden, sometimes necessary.

Cállate. - Be quiet.
(KAH-jah-teh)
🏠 Shhh... don't wake the neighbors.

Quédate quieto/quieta. - Stay still.
(KEH-dah-teh KYEH-toh/KYEH-tah)

🏠 Like a statue, but cuter.

Dime la verdad. - Tell me the truth.
(DEE-meh lah behr-DAHD)
🏠 I promise I won't get mad... maybe.

Come con la boca cerrada. - Eat with your mouth closed.
(KOH-meh kohn lah BOH-kah seh-RRAH-dah)
🏠 Nobody wants a food show.

Baja los codos de la mesa. - Take your elbows off the table.
(BAH-hah lohs KOH-dohs deh lah MEH-sah)
🏠 Manners make champions.

Siéntate aquí. - Sit here.
(SYEHN-tah-teh ah-KEE)
🏠 Next to the best company ever.

Entra a bañarte. - Go take a shower.
(EHN-trah ah bah-NYAHR-teh)
🏠 Soap is your best friend.

No toques eso. - Don't touch that.
(noh TOH-kehs EH-soh)
🏠 Danger or just sticky... either way, no.

Átate los cordones. - Tie your shoelaces.
(AH-tah-teh lohs kohr-DOH-nehs)
🏠 Before you trip in public.

Lávate los dientes. - Brush your teeth.
(LAH-bah-teh lohs DYEHN-tehs)
🏠 Your dentist approves this message.

Come tus verduras. - Eat your vegetables.
(KOH-meh toos behr-DOO-rahs)

🏠 Superpowers included.

Haz tus deberes. - Do your homework.
(AHS toos deh-BEH-rehs)
🏠 Future you will be grateful.

Ayuda a tu hermano. - Help your brother.
(ah-JOO-dah ah too ehr-MAH-noh)
🏠 Sibling points unlocked.

¡No se peleen! - Don't fight!
(NOH seh peh-LEH-ehn)
🏠 Peace treaty in the living room.

¡Ya basta! - That's enough!
(jah BAHS-tah)
🏠 The universal "parent voice."

💡 No Sabo Challenge

Do you live with your Latina mom? Record your interactions as she tells you your daily chores in Spanish. Try to recognize some of the phrases seen in this section. If you live on your own, record yourself as you clean your house and say these phrases out loud! Then, post your video on TikTok or Instagram with the hashtag #NoSaboChallenge! Look up the hashtag to check out how others clean their home.

Instagram

Subí una historia a mejores amigos. - I posted a story to close friends.
(soo-BEE OO-nah ees-TOH-ryah ah meh-HOH-rehs ah-MEE-gohs)
📱 *Mejores amigos* = green circle on Instagram, aka VIP *chisme* club.

Siempre subo fotos con filtro. - I always post photos with a filter.
(SYEHM-preh SOO-boh FOH-tohs kohn FEEL-troh)
📱 We all do, don't we?

¿Viste la publicación de Mica? - Did you see Mica's post?
(BEES-teh lah poo-blee-kah-SYOHN deh MEE-kah)
📱 You have to know the difference between *publicación* (post) and *historia* (story).

Tengo bloqueado a mi ex en Instagram - I have my ex blocked on Instagram.
(TEHN-goh-bloh-KEH-ah-doh ah mee eks ehn EENS-tah-grahm)
📱 Block button = self-care.

¿Viste el reel que te mandé? - Did you see the reel I sent you?

(BEES-teh ehl rreel keh teh mahn-DEH)
📱 Translation: "pls validate my humor."

Te envié un DM hace un rato. - I sent you a DM a while ago.
(teh ehn-BYEH oon deh EH-meh AH-seh oon RRAH-toh)
📱 You can also hear **MD** (EH-meh deh), which stands for
mensaje directo.

Siempre comparto sus publicaciones. - I always share their
posts.
(SYEHM-preh kohm-PAHR-toh soos poo-blee-kah-SYOH-
nehs)
📱 We do this for just causes and friends with small
businesses.

Mi novia tiene 15.000 seguidores. - My girlfriend has 15,000
followers.
(mee NOH-byah TYEH-neh KEEN-seh meel seh-gee-DOH-
rehs)
📱 See how, in Spanish, we use points to separate thousands
in large numbers.

Tomémonos una selfi al atardecer. - Let's take a selfie at
sunset. (toh-MEH-moh-nohs oo-nah SEHL-fee ahl ah-tahr-
deh-SEHR)
📱 Lucky for you, a *selfie* is a selfi also in Spanish.

Between Cultures: A lot of content creators from
non-English speaking countries still use English to reach
a wider audience. But the content available in Spanish is
HUGE and deeply interesting. It would be a waste to miss
out on all of that just for not speaking Spanish!

YouTube

Pongan "me gusta" al video. - Like the video.
(POHN-gahn meh GOOS-tah ahl bee-DEH-oh)
📱 Many latino moms still say ***Ponle dedito arriba*** ("Put your thumb up").

Suscríbanse a mi canal. - Subscribe to my channel.
(soos-KREE-bahn-seh ah mee kah-NAHL)
📱 Classic YouTuber outro phrase.

¿Conoces mi canal de YouTube? - Do you know my YouTube channel? (koh-NOH-sehs mee kah-NAHL deh joo-TOOB)
📱 Both "canal" and "channel" are translated as *canal* in Spanish.

Borraron mi video por copyright. - They took down my video for copyright. (boh-RRAH-rohn mee bee-DEH-oh pohr KOH-pee-rayt)
📱 As you've probably noticed, Spanish digital vocabulary has

borrowed many words from English.

Hay más de mil comentarios. - There are more than a thousand comments.
(AH-y mahs deh meel koh-mehn-TAH-ryohs)
📱 More comments = more *chismes* in the replies.

El video de Gime se volvió viral. - Gime's video went viral.
(ehl bee-DEH-oh deh HEE-meh seh bohl-BYOH bee-RAHL)
📱 Note the difference in pronunciation for *viral* in English and Spanish.

X (formerly known as Twitter)

Pedro borró el tuit de ayer. - Pedro deleted yesterday's tweet.
(PEH-droh boh-RROH ehl tweet deh ah-JEHR)
📱 If it's gone, it was probably juicy.

Doxearon a mi primo. - They doxxed my cousin.
(dohk-seh-AH-rohn ah mee PREE-moh)
📱 *Doxear*, as you've probably guessed is the Spanish version of "to dox."

¿Pero lo tuiteó o lo retuiteó? - But did he tweet it or retweet it?
(PEH-roh loh twee-teh-OH oh loh rreh-twee-teh-OH)
📱 There's a big difference here.

Denuncié la publicación por contenido ofensivo. - I reported the post for offensive content.
(deh-noon-SYEH lah poo-blee-kah-SYOHN pohr kohn-teh-NEE-doh oh-FEHN-see-boh)
📱 Don't hesitate to press the report button if you read something offensive.

WhatsApp

Escríbeme al WhatsApp. - Text me on WhatsApp.
(ehs-KREE-beh-meh ahl WAHTS-ahp)
🔄 Another option is saying **Mándame un WhatsApp**.

Te mando un audio, es más fácil. - I'll send you a voice note, it's easier.
(teh MAHN-doh oon ah-OO-dyoh ehs mahs FAH-seel)
📱 Easier for whom?

No puedo escuchar ahora. - I can't listen right now.
(noh PWEH-doh ehs-koo-CHAHR ah-OH-rah)
📱 Everyone says this but still listen to the audio anyway.

Perdón, recién veo tu mensaje. - Sorry, I just saw your message.
(pehr-DOHN reh-SYEN BEH-oh too mehn-SAH-heh)
📱 The universal lie.

¿Ya viste el grupo? - Did you check the group?
(jah BEES-teh ehl GROO-poh)
📱 Translation: "Scroll up, we planned your life without you."

Silencié el grupo por un año. - I muted the group for a year.
(see-len-SYEH ehl GROO-poh pohr oon AH-nyoh)
📱 You should do this with every WhatsApps group chat, specially the family ones!

Si entro a su chat sabrá que leí su mensaje. - If I open the chat he'll know I read his message.
(see EHN-troh ah soo chat sah-BRAH keh leh-EE soo mehn-SAH-heh)
📱 But only if you still have the double blue tick turned on...

Me dejaste en visto. - You left me on read.

(meh deh-HAHS-teh ehn BEES-toh)

🔄 In Mexico you can also hear **Me clavaste el visto**, and in Puerto Rico, **Me dejaste en azul**.

¿Quién mira los estados de WhatsApp? - Who even sees WhatsApp stories? (kyehn MEE-rah lohs ehs-TAH-dohs deh WAHTS-ahp)

📱 Well, *abuelas* and *tías*, of course!

Phone

Mi hermana se pasa todo el día scrolleando. - My sister spends all day scrolling. (mee ehr-MAH-nah seh PAH-sah TOH-doh ehl DEE-ah skroh-leh-AHN-doh)

📱 Is scroll the new cardio?

Tengo 4 horas diarias de tiempo en pantalla. - I have 4 hours of screen time.
(TEHN-goh KWAH-troh OH-rahs DYAH-ryahs deh TYE-HM-poh ehn pahn-TAH-jah)

📱 If this number is higher than 6, you should be worried!

Enciende las notificaciones en tu celular. - Turn on notifications on your phone.
(ehn-SYEHN-deh lahs noh-tee-fee-kah-SYOH-nehs ehn too seh-loo-LAHR)

📱 Translation: "Don't ghost me."

Tengo el celular en silencio. - My phone is on silent.
(TEHN-goh ehl seh-loo-LAHR ehn see-LEHN-syoh)

📱 The Latino way of ignoring chats without guilt.

Me quedé sin batería. - My battery died.
(meh keh-DEH seen bah-teh-REE-ah)

📱 Top excuse, after *Me quedé dormido*.

Ya nadie usa emojis. - Nobody uses emojis anymore.
(jah NAH-dyeh OO-sah eh-MOW-jees)
🔄 Gen Z prefers stickers, gifs, or just "💀."

Mi abuela siempre me manda spam. - My grandma always sends me spam.
(mee ah-BWEH-lah SYEHM-preh meh MAHN-dah spahm)
📱Prayer chains, *buenos días* gifs, *bendiciones*, etc.

No toques el enlace, es una estafa. - Don't click on the link, it's a scam.
(noh TOH-kehs ehl ehn-LAH-seh ehs OO-nah ehs-TAH-fah)
📱 When in doubt, ask the Latino IT department, aka, your older cousin.

No caigas en una estafa piramidal. - Don't fall for a pyramid scheme.
(noh KAHY-gahs ehn OO-nah ehs-TAH-fah pee-rah-mee-DAHL)
📱 If it sounds like easy money... it's probably a scam.

Me hackearon la cuenta. - They hacked my account.
(meh hah-keh-AH-rohn lah KWEHN-tah)
📱 This usually happens after you click on *abuela*'s spam.

Mi abuela le envió dinero a un príncipe nigeriano. - My grandma sent money to a Nigerian prince.
(mee ah-BWEH-lah leh ehn-BYOH dee-NEH-roh ah oon PREEN-see-peh nee-heh-RYAH-noh)
📱 Internet scam starter pack.

¿Nos tomarías una foto? - Would you take a picture of us?
(nohs toh-mah-REE-ahs OO-nah FOH-toh)
📱 Add *por fa* and you sound instantly more Latino.

Online (and Offline) Teasing Phrases

El talento lo persigue, pero él es más rápido - Talent chases him, but he's faster.
(ehl tah-LEHN-toh loh pehr-SEE-geh PEH-roh ehl ehs mahs RRAH-pee-doh)
📱 Perfect caption for your friend who fails but always tries.

¿Eres o te haces? - Are you dumb or just pretending?
(EH-rehs oh teh AH-sehs)
📱 Latin America's ultimate roast.

Mira quién habla. - Look who's talking.
(MEE-rah kyehn AH-blah)
📱 Use when your *primo* accuses you of the same thing he does.

¿Y por casa cómo andamos? - And at home, how are things?
(ee pohr KAH-sah KOH-moh ahn-DAH-mohs)
📱 Classic comeback when someone criticizes you.

¿Quién? ¿Quién te preguntó? - Who? Who asked you?
(kyehn kyehn teh preh-goon-TOH)
📱 Latino meme energy—shuts down any unwanted opinion.

💡 No Sabo Challenge

Go online and search for the Spanish content creators with the most followers. Watch some of their videos or read their posts, especially the comment section. Record the best comments you find and show your findings on social media! Post your video on TikTok or Instagram with the hashtag #NoSaboChallenge.

Conclusion

The rise of the *No Sabo* identity is more than just a TikTok trend or a funny meme, it represents a powerful cultural shift, where words once used as a way to tease people are being reclaimed and reimagined as symbols of pride and belonging.

This book is designed to help you embrace *español*, and to give you the confidence you need to talk to your relatives! With this goal in mind, this book has given you more than 800 phrases to talk about your everyday life, school, work, travel, shopping, social media and dating, but also phrases that cover situations particular to *latinos*, like listening to our *abuela's* sayings, having a huge gathering with family, using *telenovela* memes, and receiving orders from *mamá*.

Beyond communication, the deeper value of this book lies in identity and belonging. For many, being able to say even a few phrases in Spanish can strengthen family bonds, bring pride in cultural heritage, and open doors socially and professionally. Every phrase learned is not just about words; it's about reclaiming a connection that might have felt distant and unbridgeable.

This book reminds readers that *español* doesn't have to be perfect to be meaningful, and that we should embrace our *No sabo* culture and talk en *español sin sentir pena*, because that's how we improve and start communicating better.

In the end, this phrasebook is more than a language tool. It's an invitation to connect — with family, with culture, and with yourself. So, go take your español for a spin at a family gathering, and leave your *tías* agape!

We're happy to know you've joined the *No sabo club*, keep it up!

www.ingramcontent.com/pod-product-compliance
Lightning Source LLC
Chambersburg PA
CBHW070714130626
46553CB00005B/1987